MOVING BEYOND CHURCH GROWTH

Other titles in

PRISMS

Turn Your Church Inside Out:
Building a Community for Others
Walt Kallestad
(2001)

A Servant's Manual:
Christian Leadership for Tomorrow
Michael W. Foss
(forthcoming)

Spiritual Maturity:
Preserving Congregational Health and Balance
Frank A. Thomas
(forthcoming)

MOVING BEYOND CHURCH GROWTH

An Alternative Vision for Congregations

Mark A. Olson

Fortress Press
Minneapolis

MOVING BEYOND CHURCH GROWTH
An Alternative Vision for Congregations

Scripture quotations are from the New Revised Standard Version Bible, copyright © 1989 by the Division of Christian Education of the National Council of Churches of Christ in the United States of America. Used with permission.

Interior design: Sarah Anondson
Cover design: David Meyer

ISBN 0-8066-4346-3

Manufactured in the U.S.A.   AF 9-4346

07   06   05   04   03   02   1   2   3   4   5   6   7   8   9   10

To my family

Elaine, Brent, and Sara

Contents

Part Four: Christian Communities of the Future

INTRODUCTION

M oses stood on a hill overlooking the Jordan River. The time
of wandering in the wilderness was about to end. God's
people would soon cross over and become a landed people.
Moses had just finished a long sermon (Deuteronomy). He had
reminded the people that things would soon be different. He told
them they must imagine a new way of living faithfully, consistent
with a core story of the past yet imaginatively open to the future.
Sabbath was to be kept as it was in the wilderness. But now, as a
landed people, Sabbath would involve more than worshiping
God. It would mean spending one day trusting that God would
provide all that was needed. Such a concept of a Sabbath was not
needed in the wilderness, but when people started "making a living" on the land, it would be easy to forget who truly makes life. If
Moses were to title his sermon, he might have called it "Moving
beyond Wilderness Wandering."

Earlier, Abraham and Sarah heard God's call and obediently
journeyed into a promise. They left their home and family and
trusted God to bless them with a future. This future could not be
described in detail. It was a mystery, a vision that called forth radical faith. A memoir about the life of Abraham and Sarah might
be given the equally mysterious title "Moving beyond Ur of
Chaldees."

Jesus appeared to the disciples after his resurrection: on the
road to Emmaus, in the locked room with Thomas, on the shore
while they were cooking breakfast. These appearances announced
a new day, a new way of living, a new vision of hope. The disciples

were given no instruction book, just a promise and a vision. A collection of these experiences might be called "Moving beyond Death Fright."

The early church gathered in Jerusalem and dealt with a problem: Paul and his mission to the Gentiles. Was the gathering of people who claimed Jesus just another Jewish sect, or was this community of believers open to all? The discussion was as heated as it was difficult. Finally, the early church discerned God's will and dared to be led into uncharted territory. The report of this venture might be named "Moving beyond a Closed Church."

The church of Jesus Christ, whose character is formed by these and many other stories, often finds itself like Moses, standing on a hilltop, looking forward, and imagining what is to happen next. The church, which believes that God "goes ahead of us, not instead of us,"[1] continually asks what is beyond the present. What is God calling us to next? To be part of this discipleship community demands a lifestyle of "moving beyond."

I am convinced the church now stands on a high hill, hearing a clarion call to venture ahead in faith. The convergence of many forces makes these days pivotal for the church. The arrival of the new millennium stands as a metaphor for the new era. Nearly sixteen hundred years of "Christendom"—Constantinian Christianity—is ending.[2] Modernity, which has powerfully shaped the present understanding of existence since at least René Descartes, is now collapsing.[3] In addition, if one embraces the view of history outlined by William Strauss and Neil Howe in *The Fourth Turning*,[4] the United States will soon enter a "turning" that they call "the Crisis." Beginning in the early 2000s, we will be experiencing tremendous external challenges as a nation. We are about to enter something new.

My experience in the church also produces a similar conviction. The fragmentation of the church on every level—ecumenical, denominational, and congregational—portrays a people of God that is at once disappointed with the present assumptions and is searching for something more. It is as if God's people are standing on the banks of the Jordan, fearful and restless. They know they can't go back, but they are afraid to go ahead. They are immobilized even as they try to imagine what lies beyond. Yet there is no choice if we are to be faithful, for we are a "moving beyond" people who will be drawn into God's future.

The title of this book, *Moving beyond Church Growth*, offers a cipher for the present situation in which the church finds itself. The principles of church growth illustrate the primary assumptions of a Constantinian and modern church. I intend for this book to join the many other voices being raised that call for the church to move beyond its present assumptions, dominated by a fascination with church growth, and discern what God might be doing now in our midst.[5] Buttressing the assumptions of modernity and Constantinian Christianity that undergird church growth will only lead to more despair, disappointment, conflict, and most of all, the quieting of the witness of the gospel. To say it simply: I am convinced God's people must be open to moving beyond church growth.

I share these insights as a pastor with a passion to be in conversation with other pastors and church leaders. The primary audience is not the academic community, although I detest the anti-intellectualism that often permeates the life of pastors, church leaders, and thus congregational life as a whole. In a time when technique is claimed to be more important than content, it is essential that we strive for depth of thought. The partnerships I have experienced with the academic community as a student, adjunct professor, guest presenter, and colleague have been great gifts to me. Those who are called to the ministry of teaching and academic pursuit will be essential allies as God's people move beyond church growth.

I pursue this adventure as a pastor serving a local congregation. The focus of this book will be on congregations and pastoral leaders of congregations, but it will also address other facets of church structure (judicatory offices, national expressions, synods, and so forth) and their impact on empowering congregations to move beyond church growth.

In these postmodern times, however, bureaucratic structures will have less impact on individual congregations. Modernity assumed great generalities as truth. The broader the application of a principle, the more true it was. Modernity sought to promote transformation by offering large, overarching principles that would be applicable to all. When this understanding is applied to organizations, modernity claims that the larger the institutional expression, the more power it has to foster change. I contend that just the opposite is true. Significant congregational change will happen one congregation, one pastor, and one text at a time, not through large bureaucratic structures.

Again, I am not interested in hurling brickbats at the institution. I have served in institutional settings both as an assistant to the bishop and on a national staff. I have witnessed firsthand the pain inflicted when those outside the structure, without appreciation of the struggle, offer little but harsh criticism, and even less imagination, for solutions. Clearly, I believe much of the growth of church bureaucracies is a result of uncritical acceptance of the modern agenda. I am convinced that moving beyond church growth will demand the dismantling of many of these structures. Yet, before we begin this crusade, I encourage those of us who are local parish pastors to begin with the dismantling of the ever-expanding congregational bureaucracies that have been assumed to be normal parts of congregational life. One value I seek to uphold involves not asking others to do what I am not willing to do. For this reason, this book focuses primarily on the congregation and parish pastors and what can assist these communities of faith to live into a post-church-growth vision.

These pages are filled with the musings of one parish pastor. I serve a congregation of nearly seventeen hundred baptized members in a small Midwestern city. I am the only ordained person on staff. I preach and preside at worship almost every week. I make hospital calls, conduct funerals, perform weddings, and baptize. Teaching confirmation, Bible classes, and adult classes fills my week. I work to build a staff team with my colleagues and provide leadership for boards and committees. My days are sometimes filled with responding to those who need a visit or who are looking to be received into a community of faith. I seek to engage strangers in the ministry of the congregation by being a public presence and witness in the community. I spend time studying and imagining what God is calling this gathered people to become. I seek to communicate that vision and encourage the congregation to embrace God's call. In other words, I am a typical parish pastor. I am honored to be a parish pastor and cannot think of anything more enjoyable, rewarding, or challenging. The perspectives shared here come from my practice as a pastor and my reflections upon that practice.

These are no dispassionate principles. Rather, they are the way I seek to be a pastor and to do ministry. As a practicing pastor I am convinced the time has come for me to imagine moving beyond growth. But in a church culture in which technique and marketing are revered, I am often lonely in this quest. More than loneliness, the unintentional demeaning and sabotage of imagination often leads to profound despair and discouragement. Pastors and congregations can show signs of such despair, even when they give the illusion of being optimistic and excited. Trying harder to practice the assumptions of modernity will only exacerbate the problem. What is needed is the courage to imagine something new. This book is an invitation to others to join with me in imagining a faithful alternative.

As we begin our journey, we need to know what we mean by "church growth." What is involved in the church-growth movement and what has brought us to this place? Why the need to move on? What resources have we brought with us for the journey? Part One, then, helps us understand church growth and looks back at how we have come to this point. "Putting the Pieces Together: Toward a Definition of 'Church Growth'" asserts that the modern project has been mirrored in the church-growth movement. This section closes by recalling the postexilic struggle in Jerusalem among the priestly class—insights from a biblical crisis that might be instructive as we seek out resources for our challenging journey beyond.

Now it is time to move ahead, to act on our understandings. Part Two suggests first steps, some of which are more tentative than others. Some may lead to dead ends, and we will return to the beginning, to try again. Albert Borgmann, in his book *Crossing the Postmodern Divide,* uses the analogy of a highway map to describe modernity.[6] Road maps assume that everything can be managed. In fact, some road maps have the audacity to assume they can tell you how long it will take to travel from Chicago to Minneapolis. The world is a fixed entity, and the maps give the illusion of control and mastery. Yet we know this isn't true. Cars break down. It takes longer to travel with a toddler in the back-seat. And, of course, there are two seasons in Minnesota: winter and road repair. Road maps paint a false picture of life. Trusting road maps leads to disappointment more often than not.

Instead of a road map, Borgmann claims the compass as the analogy for postmodernity. While envisioning a destination, a compass keeps us focused toward the right direction. Life is not an interstate highway system. Life is like a wilderness. Often the journey in the wilderness does not involve straight lines, but wandering. A compass, fixed on a distant vision, allows for a circuitous way of travel, and at the same time, a confident sense of direction and movement.

The first steps proposed here are wandering. They are in many cases a reframing of dominant understandings of ministry. Hopefully, the first steps described here will lead to courage, imagination, and new ventures. Maybe we will even leave behind the road maps and the false world they portray and venture on "paths yet untrodden, through perils unknown." May we pray for "good courage, not knowing where we go, but only that [God's] hand is leading us and [God's] love supporting us."[7]

As we venture forth, a view of the congregation begins to emerge. The congregation is the most fundamental—not exclusive, but most visible—expression of God's presence in the world. In a time when other bureaucratic structures have claimed to be expressions of the church, congregations must, for the sake of the gospel, unashamedly reclaim their primacy. Responsibility accompanies such audacity. Congregations as places of worship and Sabbath-keeping are essential to moving beyond church growth. Finally, the congregations must be clear about what they are called to be. Church programming, a modern invention, must give way to a relational understanding. This will demand risk-taking and moving quickly and boldly; and embracing such a style of ministry may involve missteps and mistakes.

Part Three asserts that very few, if any, organizations move past their leaders. While not wanting to return to hierarchical models of leadership, which have been destructive to the church and its witness, if the church is to have the courage to venture forth, it must have strong leaders. A significant challenge before the church, and all of postmodern society, involves imaging the role of and practice of its leaders. Part Three seeks to provoke this conversation, which must involve not just pastors and set-apart leaders of the church but congregational members as well.

When we stand on the edge, about to enter something new, our journey requires a panoramic view of the horizon. In broad strokes, what is the direction toward which the journey must lead? Part Four of this book offers such a view. What, in broad strokes, does faithful witness to the gospel look like in a postmodern age? What is the shape of a post-Constantinian church? What does it mean to be a pastor or church leader as we move beyond church growth? Chapter 11, "Faithful Community: A Creation Myth," provides a foundational story into which God calls the church.

"The Island of Faithfulness," chapter 12, announces the dynamic character of faithful community. God's people witness boldly when they are "a people of the way." Faithful communities are drawn into God's future.

A note about the style of writing that describes this adventure: One of the challenges facing the evangelical witness of the church is to move beyond the polarities of conservative and liberal. A conservative response to the present situation would be a return to the past, most likely articulated in a propositional way, to ensure the recovery of what is right.

A liberal response would seek to address the situation with as little structure as possible. All avenues must be explored. All experience is true. For the liberal, there is no one way to proceed. As long as one proceeds with conviction, the way is true. In this book, *narrative,* or *story,* will provide an alternative to both the conservative and the liberal approaches. A narrative provides a structure, a way of ordering life and meaning. At the same time, a narrative allows for imagination and openness. A story has the wonderful ability to simultaneously provide a grounding and provoke vision.

The characters in these narratives are fictional. Yet I have been blessed with congregations that have opened their lives to me and have allowed me the honor of being their pastor. They have put up with some crazy schemes that ended in disaster. Any successes have been due to their openness to God's presence and their willingness to risk. I am the pastor I am because of St. Peter and Peace Lutheran in Garnavillo, Iowa; Valley Lutheran in Westminster, Colorado; Bethany Lutheran in Englewood, Colorado; and Zion Lutheran in Appleton, Wisconsin. In addition to these, the many congregations that have invited me into their lives as a consultant will notice many of the themes we struggled with together in these pages. Most of all, Hope Lutheran in Eau Claire, Wisconsin, endures these musings regularly. Their encouragement and willingness to move beyond church growth has made this book possible.

In addition to congregations, I have been blessed by the support of colleagues. The ideas in this book have been refined through the honest feedback of people who care deeply about the church. The ongoing day-to-day adventure of leading a congregation is the context for these musings. Tom Hamilton, Kyra Lunde, and Sue Norgaard, my partners on the staff team at Hope Lutheran, share that journey with me. They have been key to making this book both real and a reality. Ted Schroeder, Laurie Chada, Brent Olson, and Harold Rast from Fortress Press, each in different ways, have provided the editorial support to bring much-needed clarity and cohesiveness to the material.

Finally, this book is dedicated to Brent, Sara, and Elaine. I am aware that my children, Brent and Sara, challenge me to "move beyond" in ways I don't likely even know. Elaine, my wife of nearly thirty years, shows more courage and conviction than she knows. She is always exploring where God might be leading her and us. If and when this book touches a nerve, offers a challenge, or grants the gift of encouragement, it is likely their wisdom, knowledge, passion, and love for the church and the gospel that you will be experiencing. I cannot imagine moving anywhere without my family near my side.

A community gathered around the biblical story responds to the compelling call to embrace God's future. Abraham and Sarah, Moses, and the prophets are people who encounter God coming to them from beyond the present and calling them to pilgrimage ahead; they are a post-church-growth people. Jesus breaks into the world as the incarnation of God's unfailing promise. He calls the church to be disciples and to live into that future promise. At the same time, a faithful pilgrim community is a historical people. God works in and through history. Even as we move beyond the present, claiming the gifts of the past, of tradition, is all the more important. We must not deny the gifts we have received from the modern era of the church. Modernity has left a lasting legacy with many resources from which to draw. Sixteen hundred years of Constantinian Christianity has produced many powerful means to witness to the gospel. The challenge for the church today is to courageously claim the future and reverently remember God's activity in the past. A church that dares to move beyond church growth boldly accepts this challenge.

1

PUTTING THE PIECES TOGETHER: TOWARD A DEFINITION OF CHURCH GROWTH

It's a great children's toy: a picture puzzle made of ten sturdy wooden interlocking pieces. What is so special about this particular puzzle is that it is two puzzles in one. As you put together the puzzle and complete the picture on one side, you create another picture on the back.

On one side, the puzzle reveals a farmstead: a house, a barn, fields, a tractor, and a fenced pasture. The other side holds a more detailed picture. This side pictures the interior of the barn, a cow in a stall, a cat in the corner, a dog at the door, pigs in their pen, chickens eating corn from the floor, pigeons in the rafters, and a farmer pitching hay.

The simple joy of the puzzle includes the excitement of completing two projects at once. By completing one side, you finish the other.

The relationship of the church growth movement and the modernity project mirrors this two-sided puzzle. As the pieces of one come together, the other finds expression as well. As the principles of modernity are pieced together and then applied to the church, the picture that emerges is the church growth movement. This picture dominates the present understanding of congregational life in the United States.

In this chapter, I will describe the ten pieces of the puzzle, the ten principles of modernity that, when put together, reveal the modern mind.[1] At the same time, I will flip each piece over and discuss how these principles look when they are expressed in congregational life. By the end of the chapter, I hope to complete the puzzle by creating a definition of modernity and church growth.

Piece One: The roots of modernity reach beyond what is usually assigned as the beginning of this period: the Enlightenment. The Renaissance, as it claimed for humankind a position of centrality in reality and thus demoted God, provided modernity's origin. Francis Bacon exemplified this by his assertion that humans could exercise power over nature and uncover nature's deepest secrets.

Turning this piece of the puzzle over, the church growth movement also originated earlier than when it came to full expression in North America. The Protestant Reformation opened the door to a more humanistic understanding of faith. Using the new intellectual tools becoming available to them, the reformers sought to uncover the meaning of faith and bring the church out of the shadows of mystery. Combined with the forces of the emerging nation-state, the church as the authoritative center of reality, especially the Roman Catholic Church in the West, came to be questioned. This questioning inevitably drew humankind into the shadow and demystified the church and its understanding of reality.

Piece Two: The Enlightenment, which took place after the Thirty Years' War, continued the movement that had begun in the Renaissance. Once humankind was lifted to the center of reality, the individual taking center stage became the next logical step. The philosopher René Descartes responded to the anxiety and doubt of his age;[2] he took control through asserting the primacy of the thinking self: "I think; therefore I am." The cognitive enterprise of the individual defined reality. The church growth side of this piece shows the work of Peter Wagner, one of the key founders of the church growth movement. Beginning in the middle of the twentieth century, Wagner acted upon his missionary passion for expanding the church in North America. One of the key convictions undergirding his work involved the claim that the gospel of Jesus Christ meets people's needs. The church must address real human needs. When this happens, the church will grow. The needs most clearly identified in this process were individual needs. This development was a shift so significant that now it is hard to recall when individual needs were not the key to church life. The church growth movement, being the flip side of the modern project, turned the church's primary focus from God to the individual human being.[3]

Piece Three: Sir Isaac Newton added a scientific framework to the modern project. Newton understood the world as a machine governed by rules and regularity. The challenge for the individual was to know the machine, its rules, and its regularity so thoroughly that the individual could control, and even modify and recreate, the machine known as existence. Thus, when existence fails, when it does not satisfy the desire of the individual, it must, like any machine, be fixed. Furthermore, modernity believes that only individuals can fix the machine. The call, the vocation, of the modern individual is to fix what is broken and to make life work.

The other side of this puzzle piece shows the sciences appropriated by the church. The social sciences provided the mechanism for fixing what was broken and making life work in the church. Church leaders began to use sociology, psychology, pedagogical studies, and organizational development to tune the church's engine of life. In addition, the careful work being done in linguistics, anthropology, sociology of religion, and the literary fields refocused the church's life. In Bible study, the historical-critical method dismantled the text in order to understand it. In congregational life, congregations were encouraged to divide their functions and then provide mission statements, goals, and objectives for each function. A mechanistic view characterized every function of the church. Christian education, church administration, and pastoral care and counseling all embraced these modern sciences and sought to develop greater competencies in these fields. If the church could engineer itself as a machine that would serve individuals perfectly, this would provide salvation and a full and happy life.

The church growth movement became a science unto itself by recasting the science of marketing for the purpose of membership recruitment. Surveys, needs analysis, and locating market niches have become common components of the church's life. Customer satisfaction, loyalty, and retention strategies are taught to the church by the most sophisticated practitioners of the marketing industry. Psychological profiling and personality inventories abound as ways to enhance the effectiveness of everything from church boards, to preaching, to personal devotional life. A mechanistic assumption undergirds all these endeavors. A scientific framework offers the promise that with enough time, energy, insight, and resources, the church can fix any problem, especially any individual distress or dis-ease. The modern church, a church-growth church, would call the fulfillment of that promise salvation. Modern salvation is living a life that works. Sin, from which the church promises release, is that which wrecks the machine and causes breakdowns.

For three hundred years or more, modernity has been about the task of perfecting life. The compelling agenda has been to explore and redefine a person as autonomous, rational, and master of the existence machine. The rest of the pieces in this simple puzzle portray the philosophical principles fueling the massive and fully encompassing project of modernity.

Piece Four: This piece shows the modern zeal for probing the human intellect as the key to unlocking the secrets of the universe. Once we know the universe, we can then own and rule it.

Modernity optimistically assumes that such knowledge and domination of existence will make life better. In the modern age, this principle has been applied to everything from the environment, to the economy, to the psyche, to the human body. The more humans can learn, the more they can master themselves and the universe, and their efforts will result in their own happiness.

The other side of this piece should surprise no one; modern congregational life governs itself by this principle. Teaching often dominates the focus of the congregational enterprise. Even worship takes on a didactic character. Preaching becomes teaching. The Bible becomes a guide, a manual for living. Jesus is a hero or mentor. Helping people master the concept of faith is a primary endeavor. How-to classes and programs permeate modern congregations. The ability to connect to everyday life, to be relevant, is of the highest value.

Under the modern mystique, providing effective leadership for a modern congregation involves communicating effectively, which means making things clear and rational. If fostering change creates conflict, usually the blame falls on the presentation of the issue, not the content of the idea itself. People say they just didn't know enough, were not taught well enough. Implied in this response is that good leaders would teach in such a way that all conflict and discomfort would be avoided. A modern church-growth congregation focuses on knowledge and providing intellectual means for unlocking the secrets of the universe, thus mastering existence.

Piece Five: Modernity's encompassing pursuit of knowledge, accompanied by the assumption that such knowledge will lead to mastery of life itself, leads to the rational managing of life through technology. If we hold a mechanistic understanding of life, we must then passionately commit ourselves to mastering the machine in order to ensure that it works. This passion leads to an encompassing trust in technology. Whereas knowledge once focused on ideas, concepts, and playful imagination, modern knowledge seeks competence, control, and efficiency, all of which are possible by the use of and unquestioned belief in technology.

Modern congregational life embraces this obsession with technology and technique. At gatherings of pastors and leaders, there is little conversation about vision or even theology. The latest computer program, sound system, or programmatic technique receive concentrated attention. Pastors leave these meetings lusting after the next technological fix that will make their congregation work better. A whole industry has grown up to provide helps (a softer term for techniques) for preaching, premarital counseling, youth ministry, stewardship, personal devotional life, and any other dimension of church life. The advent of the Internet and the proliferation of information only exacerbates the insatiable need for more techniques, more technologies. This frenzied pursuit of technique is grounded in the assumption that the more knowledge and competency one has, the more one can master life, even church life.[4]

Piece Six: Delving more deeply into the modern commitment to knowledge, three characteristics are clear: modern knowledge is certain, objective, and good.

The next piece in our modern puzzle depicts the characteristic of certainty. To know something is to be certain of it. To know someone is to be certain of him or her. Certainty must be verifiable when life is understood mechanistically. Certainty involves a lack of doubt, questioning, or mystery. The proof of the certainty of something is in what it does or what it accomplishes, or to say it in another way, what it masters and controls.

The flip side of this piece of the puzzle shows a church-growth church caught in a difficult dilemma. A primary value of the church is faith. Faith is trust, and trust is possible only in the absence of certainty. Yet the modern credo demanding certain knowledge makes this view difficult, if not impossible, to hold. Either one denies the dominant modern worldview, or one foregoes a basic tenet of belief. Or, as church growth has done, one reframes the issue and focuses instead on something more concrete, the "hurts and hopes"[5] of humankind. Those things that cannot be verifiable are diminished, and those that are real and rational are embraced. So the Bible is used only in ways that can be defended rationally. It becomes a guidebook and provides wisdom and inspiration. Church-growth churches dismiss the sacraments as being too mysterious and too great a leap for the modern mind. Pastors, once the habitat of the divine,[6] come to see themselves as just another one of the helping professions that deal with real, certain, human needs. In the modern age, the church-growth church deals with what it can know for sure: life in the here and now. Everything else demands faith, and faith cannot be known with certainty. What cannot be known is not real, and thus is false and meaningless.

Piece Seven: Along with certainty, another modern characteristic of knowledge is objectivity. In modernity, a person assumes one can know and act without being conditioned by extraneous forces. Objectivity is an essential component of the modern project. The goal of the individual finding happiness through mastering something demands that the knower be dispassionate and outside the influence of what is being known.

This objective knowledge also applies to history. For the modern person, history is of little concern, because it has no impact on the present. The same may be said for the future. Future hopes and impending future crises must not influence the present objective knowledge. "Seize the day" is more than just a motto; it is an essential mind-set for supporting the modern value of objective, dispassionate knowledge.

The modern church-growth church acts out this characteristic of objectivity, denying salvation history and God's people as a historical people. If we allow the here and now to be influenced by the past, we lose the objectivity of the present. The modern church silences the eschatological dimensions of the Christian story. To lose oneself to the future and to be influenced by what is characterized as pie-in-the-sky visions compromises objectivity. A modern church must be grounded in the here and now and must not be molded by history or by future promises. To be true and real is to be unconditionally present.

Piece Eight: Objectivity promotes specialization. Life is complex, and the quest for dispassionate, objective knowledge is impossible. For someone to be competent, to have intellectual mastery over some aspect of life seen as a machine, one must specialize. Thus, for the modern age, the more specialized the knowledge, the more trusted it is. Generalists lose credibility when dealing with some aspects of life, because they become too influenced by broader implications.

This specialization gets acted out in the church-growth church at many levels. A philosophy of specialization separates method and content. Meaning and content now are regularly disconnected from technique. Thus it is possible for specialists in the church to have little or no grounding in the whole of the tradition. For example, a therapist who was a practicing Buddhist was hired in a Christian counseling center. When asked about it, the organization defended itself by pointing to her undeniable abilities as a therapist. They assumed that because she was competent, she would be dispassionate and objective. The issues of Christian belief were outside her influence. The same issues arise with marketing techniques, worship style, and morality. In the modern church, one arena of life does not have any impact on another, and this is considered a virtue.

Specialization can be seen in more visible ways. Church-growth churches compartmentalize congregational life. For example, the congregation's functions—such as worship, learning, service, support, and caring—involve setting goals and objectives for each function and hiring specialized staff. Pastoral selection committees seek out pastors who are specialists and can remain focused (read: objective) on the present task at hand. Their ability to avoid the distractions (read: influence) of other agendas determines the level of their success.

Specialization also works its way into worship. Worship in the church-growth church seeks to meet the specialized needs of certain niche groups. The whole of the Christian tradition is compromised by this sought-after objectivity. The variety of worship styles, even within one congregation, mirrors the variety of staff and programs.

Piece Nine: The modern landscape is colored by the assumption that knowledge is certain, objective, and good. It unquestioningly embraces the notion of the inherent goodness of knowledge. More knowledge will lead to more certainty, more objectivity, and thus to a greater mastery of the world and of the whole self. The deeply ingrained belief in the goodness of knowledge fuels the unbridled optimism characteristic of the modern world, especially in North America.[7] The increasing availability of information, the insatiable appetite for data, and the technological resources to access and manage all this knowledge embolden such an optimistic view of the future that any opposing voices are dismissed as pathological. In the modern age, a healthy individual sees the world as evolving and exploding with ever-new insights and revelations. The abundant growth of knowledge ensures good results. Only those who are misinformed or who are paranoid about the future would see it otherwise.

The church-growth church applies the idea of the inherent goodness of knowledge and its resultant optimism to its message and its practice. Bigger barns, both figurative and literal, signify success and also validate the goodness of the ministry. Optimism leads to growth. Growth proves the goodness, even faithfulness, of ministry. Because it is impossible to quantify the growth of faith (an oxymoron), the modern church has skillfully adapted statistical and measurable tools to assess knowledge, optimism, and goodness. In the modern church, what cannot be counted cannot be blessed. A whole new industry has emerged around the analysis of statistical reports, financial ledgers, and other computable functions of the church. The reason such emphasis is placed upon this is the profound belief that knowledge is good. With all the knowledge available, all the goodness available, any church open to this new knowledge must overflow with tremendous optimism. For the modern church, only sloth or negative thinking—modern sins—could thwart the growth God wants to give.

Piece Ten: Finally, individual freedom, the centerpiece that holds the puzzle together, fits snugly into place. The modern age has been a quest for freedom. True modern freedom demands the hard work of distancing oneself from all influences that compromise objectivity. This happens through the hyperactive accumulation of knowledge, skills, and resources that ensure self-sufficiency. To be free is to be outside any control or demand. To be free is to be the master of one's destiny. This quest for autonomy applies to both the internal and external dimensions of life. A free individual is not bound by the psychological, the spiritual, or the traditional. The modern agenda seeks completion in the free individual, the master of life.

Church growth also has individual freedom as the centerpiece of its life. Individual faith takes precedence over personal faith. The church-growth church seeks to unleash people from all the trappings that inhibit their freedom. Tradition, doctrine, loyalty, and sacrifice only imprison the individual. The absence of these defining elements of congregational life means the church becomes a purveyor of whatever the individuals desire. The church, now focused around and committed to the free individual, dispenses commodities to ensure and further enhance this freedom. The irony of the mission of the modern church is that its success will mean its demise. Finally, the individual will be set free even from the influence and necessity of the church.

A Picture Emerges

The puzzle is now complete. On one side of the puzzle, this rendering of modern life is clear: humankind is asserting the ability to unlock secrets that before were thought to be beyond understanding. A careful look reveals the individual, and even more specifically, the individual mind, as the core of existence. "I think, therefore I am" resounds as the creed of the modern age. This grounding promoted the envisioning of life, all of life, as mechanistic. Modernity embraces the individual as a rational presence able to master the world through scientific methodologies. This results in an unquestioned commitment to technology and technique.

This picture of modernity portrays knowledge, the key element of the modern project, as certain, objective, and good. The narrower the specialty, the more it is certain, objective, and good. Life is divided into different arenas, and no unifying story exists to hold it together.

Finally, the puzzle boldly announces the goal of the modern agenda. Modernity seeks freedom for the individual. A fully modern person will be autonomous and above the influence of community or tradition. The individual will be the master of their own destiny.

The completion of the modern picture also puts all the pieces together for asserting a definition of church growth. Church growth places the hurts and hopes of humankind at the center of the church's life. Such an audacious move pushes God toward the edge. Like modernity, humankind finds its expression in the individual. Individual hurts and hopes claim the attention of a church-growth church. The faith of individuals is cognitive, mechanistic, and reliant on technique and technology. The modern church exists as a tool for individual faith development, using the social sciences as its foundation.

The social sciences, a modern creation, prompt the church to evaluate the effectiveness of its ministry using a modern understanding of knowledge. The modern church must proclaim a message that is certain, objective, beyond influence, and optimistic. A church-growth church must uplift, inspire, and motivate an ever-increasing commitment to progress. An effective ministry by a modern church can be seen in the individual lives of its members. Their felt needs are met, they are happy, and every day they become more and more autonomous and free. The church-growth church provides the tools for them to become masters of their own destinies.

What Does It Mean?

The puzzle has been put together, taken apart, and put together again and again over the past three hundred or more years. As of late, the pieces are not fitting as snugly as they once did. The corners are becoming worn, and the once-clear images are fading. The modern view is breaking apart, and with it, the flip side picture of church growth is being dismantled as well.

Maybe this is happening because the individual, the center-piece of the puzzle, is getting tired of holding it all together. Maybe the weight is too great to bear alone. Maybe being free and autonomous is just another way of being alone and lonely.

Maybe the puzzle no longer holds together because the heaping doses of disappointment with technique and technology place pressure on the edges. Maybe what Walter Wink said about the historical-critical method of biblical study applies to the whole of modernity and the church. Wink claimed that the historical-critical method left us bankrupt. It did not produce benefits worthy of the investment.[8]

Maybe the world has grown up, and a simple puzzle no longer can hold the imagination. Maybe the modern individual has come to accept that there are mysteries beyond understanding. Maybe all of life is not a machine that can be torn apart, tuned up, greased, and then fixed. Maybe life doesn't work.

Maybe the puzzle has lost its commanding presence because putting it together is no longer fun. Maybe the optimism, which has denial as a significant component, can no longer be defended. The hard fall from an addiction to optimism is a profoundly painful and frightening crash. The epidemic of despair and depression now rampant in the modern world, the massive use of medications to soften the blow, indicate this truth.

Maybe the cost of the commodification of all existence has become too high. Everything has a price, and thus everything and everyone can be purchased. Sacredness, dignity, and authenticity are lost. Meaninglessness and purposelessness are the result. Violence manifests itself as an attempt to secure what cannot be bought at any price.

Or maybe, just maybe, the God who created the world from chaos, who delivered the Hebrews from Egypt, who brought home the exiles from Babylon, plans to act yet again. Maybe the God who sent Jesus to redeem the world, all creation, and to save all of life, keeps on creating even through this time. Maybe God, who the modern project relegated to the edge and claimed as unnecessary, longs again to be Immanuel, "God with us." Maybe God is breaking apart the modern puzzle and the church-growth church so that God might bring forth a new definition, a new way of being, a new people, a new creation, and new shalom.

God grant us, in the name of Jesus, and by the power of the Spirit, the grace to endure the tearing apart of the modern puzzle and the dismantling of the church-growth church so that we, and all creation, might be defined again in a new way, according to God's will.

2

ECHOES OF AN ANCIENT CONFLICT

Historical Note: Many Yahwists greeted the rise of Cyrus to a position of hegemony with enthusiasm and hope for the future, especially when it became clear that he would support the return of Jewish exiles to Jerusalem and the restoration of the cult (the Edict of Cyrus, 538 B.C.E.). As high hopes collided with the harsh realities of rebuilding a devastated land, however, the frustration and despair began to descend like a shroud over the returnees. The problem was compounded by tension between rival groups as they struggled for control over the building of temple and community. The Zadokite priestly party was able to repress the dissident group coming to expression in Isaiah 56-66 and, with the support of the prophets Haggai and Zechariah, was able to rebuild the temple between 520 and 515 B.C.E. But a deep wound had torn into the tissue of the community, setting the stage for continued struggle between the Zadokites and the Levites, as well as between those with pragmatic and those with visionary predilections throughout the Second Temple Period.[1]

The trip from the headquarters to the conference site was a long day's drive. Neither of them could imagine being in each other's presence for this amount of time, but when the Big Guy speaks, you listen.

A while back they had been summoned into Yahweh's presence, and they were told, not asked, that they must attend a conference entitled, "From Rubble to Renewal: Raising Up a Vital, Alive Church." Neither of them wanted to attend. And if they had to go, going as partners was not a pleasant thought. But the instructions were clear. They must attend, and they must go together, stay together, and talk together about what they would see and hear. Yahweh was firm about this. It was time for these two opponents, so different yet both such an important part of God's activity in the world, to work things through.

So it was that Trito-Isaiah (called Trito for short) and Zadok were in a car lumbering across the Kansas plains, heading south and west. For the first few hours, they said nothing to each other. But soon they wearied of country music on the radio and the lack of variety in the landscape, so they made some tentative gestures in communication. It had been a long time since they had spoken a civil word to each other.

Trito began to speak in a fanciful and nostalgic voice, a tone that drove Zadok crazy. Trito spoke of how this countryside with its seemingly endless vacantness reminded him of how it felt to be an exile, to be alone and cut off. Although the landscape was different, the inner feeling was the same. No matter what direction he looked, he could not see home.

Zadok was driving. (He did most of the driving, having more than a passing need for control.) Zadok held on to the steering wheel, looked straight ahead, and said nothing. Even as he was open to any kind of stimulation other than tumbleweeds and another song about a lost love, he was not sure he wanted to encourage Trito's retelling of the hard times in Babylon. That was past, and it must be forgotten. It was time to deal with the here and now.

Trito, however, needed no encouragement, and in the absence of any request to be quiet, he continued to speak to the windshield, not looking for or expecting a response from Zadok. "Someone said about the Great Plains that the plains 'have room for history.' It is an amazing paradox that in the midst of this emptiness I find myself full of visions and hopes and dreams. It was the same in Babylon."

Trito's voice had a sing-song kind of feel it to it. To Zadok, Trito's words and the effect of his voice were like cotton candy: full of air and little substance.

Yet Trito either did not notice or did not pay attention to Zadok's displeasure. He continued on.

"In Babylon, we felt like a people lost and discarded. It was so easy, and so often the case, that we felt and lived with great despair. Our world had literally fallen around us, and we now lived with the memory of Jerusalem being nothing more than a pile of rubble. We wondered if we had been abandoned and forgotten. Maybe Yahweh had lost power and the Babylonian gods were in charge. Yet, even in our despair, or maybe because of our emptiness and hopelessness, God spoke to us. God spoke through images of a suffering servant who, through his patient presence, would be a blessing and a source of redemption. God encouraged us to remember God's promise that we are a chosen people. God even expanded God's promises to include all creation. God revealed to us the wonder of 'shalom', a time when the threat of chaos would no longer exist, and redemption would no longer be an experience for the future, but a present reality. In all these images, spoken to us in the midst of emptiness and bondage, God spoke of reconciling God's people to God's self."

Like a mist that makes everything wet yet cannot be felt as it falls, Trito spoke his visions. They did not seem to have any substance, just a pervasive presence. For what seemed like hours, he spoke; like a poet, he spoke of his time in Babylon and how the emptiness of the plains reminded him of that experience.

Finally, Zadok could take it no longer. They were driving through the very tip of the panhandle of Texas on their way toward New Mexico when Zadok spoke out. When Trito was taking a breath, Zadok asked succinctly, "What did God tell you to do? What was the plan?"

Trito looked at Zadok with a startled and blank stare. First of all, he was surprised that Zadok had spoken at all. Second, the question he asked had never occurred to Trito. For a while there was silence in the car. Finally, after they were into New Mexico a number of miles, Trito responded.

"God asked us to trust the vision. That was the plan. Worship God and trust the vision. Let the vision shape our future. Let the vision direct our way. Let the vision of the highway home be our hope and identity and life. That was the plan."

Now it was Zadok's turn to respond with more than a questioning look. Such a response was beyond unintelligible; it was crazy. In fact, the more Zadok thought about it, the more it seemed downright dangerous.

Zadok was about to cry out in a scathing attack on this visionary mumbo-jumbo, but then the ever-present practical side of him took over. He realized they had many more hours to travel. Better to be disciplined and swallow his anger than to cause a mess in the close quarters of a car with many miles yet to be traveled. But he did offer a harshly whispered response that was a curse of Yahweh for demanding he spend this time with a traveling companion who had clouds for brains.

Maybe it was the curse, or maybe it was a coincidence, but just then they heard a *pop,* and the car began to rattle and pull to the right. The right front tire had blown. Zadok, ever in control, guided the car carefully to the shoulder of the road and took charge. In no time at all, Zadok had the tire jack and the spare tire out of the car. He popped the hubcap off the torn tire and began to work on the lug nuts. Meanwhile, Trito was looking at the equally expansive sky and desert, taking deep breaths of the dry, clear air. Zadok looked at him, muttered something about being useless, and worked at loosening the nuts.

All the lug nuts were removed and placed in the hubcap, which now functioned as a bowl. All, that is, except one. For some reason, in spite of great effort, he could not loosen one of the nuts. Finally, exhausted, he decided to rest before he tried again. Frustrated and weary, Zadok sat on a rock on the side of the road and looked north. Before him was nothing but sand, rocks, scrub trees, and tumbleweeds. It was a land of nothing and clearly a place where little or nothing worked. He looked back at the car lifted high on the tire jack, a car as useless as the land. As if to confirm his appraisal of the land, he noticed, off the in the distance, a grove of trees that offered a splash of green to the otherwise beige landscape. Looking closer, he noticed a dilapidated farmstead; a windmill was the only thing standing, and it wasn't even working. A car passed by on the road but did not stop. It caused Zadok's attention to move back and forth between the useless car and the rubble of the farmstead. Then Zadok, unaware that Trito was sitting on the ground near him, began to speak to himself.

"Just like Jerusalem. This reminds me of Jerusalem after the exiles returned. The whole city was useless. Not one stone was left upon another. The exiles returned, thrilled to be home. God had kept God's promise, and they were filled with visions of God working in this world. They had grand visions but no plan. They were filled with energy and excitement but had no way to make it practical. They had traveled home on the highway God had told them about, but now they were stuck, like a car with a flat tire. Jerusalem was a mess, and no fanciful thinking would help. What was needed was a plan of action."

Zadok was about to go on when he heard a large semi truck begin to gear down and move toward a stop behind the car. Zadok got up and watched as a large man slowly unloaded himself from the cab. He was about as wide as he was tall, with a full head of hair under a Mack Truck baseball cap. The truck driver looked at Zadok and said, "Looks like you got trouble." He looked carefully at the blown tire still attached by the one lug nut and immediately understood the problem. Without a word he went to get some spray lubricant and a longer tire wrench. With a quick spray and just a little of his weight on the wrench, the nut was loose. Then, just to make sure the job was finished, he put on the spare, as easily as if he were playing with Tinker Toys.

As the truck driver closed the trunk of the car, he looked at Zadok and Trito and said, "Don't get me wrong. I didn't do this because I am a nice guy or anything. I help people because things work better when the road is clean. I'm not nice, just practical. Just doin' my job." Then he hoisted himself back into the truck cab, and off he went.

Down the road a bit, Trito broke the silence and said, "Thank God for the trucker. He really helped. He seemed like a nice guy, though he didn't want to admit it."

Zadok was thinking about the abandoned farmstead and the rubble of Jerusalem. "Sometimes it's not a matter of being nice; sometimes you just have to do things in order to, like the trucker said, 'make things work.'"

It was clear to Trito that Zadok was not just speaking about the trucker, but also about himself. This became more evident as Zadok continued.

"The exiles, when they returned, were so caught up in the wonder of what God had done and in their visions of what God was doing that they were useless. They were nice people, good folk, but in the midst of the chaos of a ruined city, they were good for little or nothing. So some of us had to forget about being nice and retelling visions and gathering for fanciful discussions. Some of us had to take charge. For the good of all the people, we did this. For the sake of the holy city of Jerusalem, we did this. As a faithful service to God, we did this. It was not always nice, but it was the right and practical thing to do."

Zadok was tightly clutching the steering wheel. His forehead was tense. This remembering was painful work for him. "We decided that we, the Zadokite priests, must take control and be in charge. It was not always nice and pleasant, but if anything was going to be accomplished, we decided we must remove the Levites and their visionary friends from power. There was a temple to build and a city to reconstruct. It was time for practical leadership."

"And we decided all this talk of the exiles about a universal vision of God's mission through Israel must be set aside. It was impractical and counterproductive, and efficient production was what we needed. Instead of talking about the redemption of all creation, we focused on ourselves and the pragmatic issues of day-to-day life and making this city, this nation, work. All that fluffy talk about a grand vision was nice for evening parties, but when it came to getting things done, we needed to focus on our own. Addressing immediate needs is what motivates people. And we were realistic, so we compromised a little bit and accommodated the Persian emperor. We knew it was risky, but you have to make some tough decisions sometimes. What would it hurt us if we did not flaunt the sovereignty of Yahweh in the face of the emperor? We had too much work to do to fight the empire as well as rebuild a people. The visionaries were upset about this. They would talk about thinking in the long term, not about the immediate situation. Yet it was the immediate problems that faced us each day. This was not the time to work on lofty ideals of purity and holiness. This was the time to be practical. It was practical to avoid angering the emperor and to accommodate the realities of the world as it is."

A few more miles down the road and Zadok finished his historical review with a brief summary. "Sometimes you have to be more than nice; you have to take charge. Sometimes you have to forsake the big issues of the world and take care of your own. Sometimes you have to compromise and accommodate. Sometimes you just have to be practical about it all."

For a long while the car was silent. Only the sound of the tires on the New Mexico and Arizona interstate was heard. Both Zadok and Trito were peering out of the windows at the desert landscape and thinking of those post-exilic days in Jerusalem.

Finally, Trito spoke, as if he were continuing a conversation that hadn't ended: "And you succeeded."

"Yes," Zadok said matter-of-factly and proudly. "Miraculously, we rebuilt Jerusalem and the Temple. We restored the nation of Israel."

"And you succeeded," Trito responded with a hint of bitterness and sorrow in his voice. "You succeeded in dismissing the Levites and dismantling the ancient tradition of that tribe of priests. You succeeded in quieting the long-held universal vision of God's redemption of all the world, and instead turned Israel's focus on itself. Yes, you succeeded in finding a way to compromise the lordship of Yahweh so you could be friends with the empire."

Then, sarcastically, Trito said, "Congratulations on your success."

Again, the pragmatic Zadok considered getting into a debate but was wearied both by the drive and the company. Better to hold in his anger and keep his eyes on the road.

They drove into the expansive valley that held Phoenix. Zadok looked upon the sprawling metroplex and was awed by the planning and organization that must have gone into making it a reality. Trito looked at the cloud of colored air and the desert turned into pavement and wondered if all the places of desert emptiness, places for visions, would soon become shopping malls and interstate highways. The conference, "From Rubble to Renewal: Raising Up a Vital Church," was being held at a megachurch complex on the outskirts of town. As they pulled into the parking lot, they were both silent, and each saw something different.

Zadok saw a practical and efficient facility. He was impressed by the simplicity of the structure—no frills or extras—and at the same time, it was clear that the technology was state-of-the-art. Zadok was excited to learn how to make such a place a reality. He imagined the people who gathered in this place likely reflected their building. They were a pragmatic people who spent time focusing on the here-and-now and how to make life work. One could feel a sense of urgency. This was a place of activity. This was his kind of place and his kind of people. He could tell just by looking at the building. He could feel it in the air.

Trito noticed what was absent. There were few or no symbols or art. The building had no real character. It could have been a warehouse, a concert hall, or a library. It was functional. He had to admit that it had a welcoming feeling. It felt easily accessible, both physically and emotionally. Yet Trito wondered what they were being invited into. As they walked up the sidewalk to the outdoor gazebo, the information center that was in the middle of the campus of buildings, Trito felt like his view of life was being narrowed. This feeling brought back memories. At first he couldn't recall where he had felt like this before. Then he figured it out. It was when he, with the other exiles, walked into Jerusalem after being set free. He felt the grand vision of God's activity in the world being threatened. He was as frightened now as he had been then.

The two-and-a-half-day conference was divided into three sections. First would be an analysis of the present situation in which the church found itself. Second would be some presentations concerning some conceptual foundations for how to be successful in this present environment. Lastly, and taking almost half the conference, participants could be involved in hands-on, practical workshops led by those who had "mastered the times" and were proven successes at raising up vital churches. Remembering Yahweh's specific instructions, they sat together and listened to the opening presentations. Following the first presentations, they went out to lunch and talked. It was a miracle of sorts. They found agreement. They were so excited about this newfound common ground that they clinked their water glasses and toasted this rare and memorable occasion.

The presentations were entitled: "State of the Church in North America." The message was clear. The present state of the church could be described as an institution dealing with its collapse. This was particularly true of the mainline denominations that had been such a prominent presence in the United States and Canada. These denominations no longer could claim the title *mainline*, but were now *sidelined*. They were dying institutions that considered it a success if they lost fewer members than they had the previous years. In addition, even though the community-church movement showed signs of growth, the total number of people who regularly worshiped in a Christian church of any denomination (or nondenomination) was not growing. Pluralism marked the religious landscape as never before. World religions were finding North America fertile soil for growth. In addition, the spirituality movement, with few or no institutional structures, was growing: just look at the sales of books and tapes and the number of participants. Zadok summarized succinctly what had been said at these opening sessions. He proclaimed, and Trito nodded his head in agreement, "Plain and simple: the Christian church is being humiliated."[2] Following this verdict, they both ate their lunch quietly. Each of them was thinking back to a time they had experienced this humiliation before. Each was thinking back to Jerusalem lying in rubble after the Exile. Each recalled the devastation of seeing the Holy City of God with not one brick left upon another. Each felt the pain of those dark days so many years ago.

But, other than a few times when they agreed on what kind of food they wanted to eat, this was the last time they found common ground. Agreeing on the nature of the problem was not an issue. Agreeing about how to respond was another thing altogether. It was clear to both of them that what divided them was not just a matter of taste, technique, semantics, or pride. The deep rift between them was foundational. On the second night, as they were about to turn out the lights in their hotel room, Trito stated their difference most clearly. It was a miracle, but what he said they both affirmed. Trito said carefully, "The church is being humiliated. On this we agree. You are eager to find some way to restore the church to its previous glory by repairing what is broken and making it work again. I also long for the church to enjoy a glory of sorts, though it may look different than your vision of glory. I believe the only way to address this longing is to enter the humiliation more fully and see it as a gift."

After a moment or two of thoughtful silence, Zadok reached out and shut off the light. As he rolled over in bed, he said, "Another thing that we agree on. You describe the source of our differences perfectly." Then he mused sarcastically, "Enter the humiliation more fully. You've got to be kidding. Even if you chose this path, practically speaking, how would you do it?"

The conference followed its format with regimented precision. The second part, dealing in conceptual ways about how the church might respond, engaged Trito but bored Zadok. The reason these presentation kept Trito hooked at all was that they made him so angry. The presenters used all sorts of sociological and psychological methodologies and language systems to assert a plan for how to proceed. It was basic marketing principles. One session was even led by a representative from a major theme park who talked about customer satisfaction, creating a positive environment, and how to be imaginative and creative so people will like you. All Trito could think about during these presentations was the strategy of the Babylonians while they were in Exile. The Babylonians did not want to annihilate the Israelites. Their plan was to assimilate them. The major weapon for assimilation is marketing. Convince those you wish to domesticate through subtle and consistent coercion. Seduce them into forgetting who they are and, through supposedly addressing their needs, redefine their character as your own. What he heard at the conference sounded just like the babble of Babylon. As he watched those around him being led down this path, he wanted to stand up and shout, "Don't forget who you are. You are people with a peculiar and particular vision. Don't let them take it away from you. Trust the vision and the God who called you into it. Be careful. This all may sound innocent, but it is dangerous, very dangerous to your soul."

Zadok did not find himself caught up much in these presentations. For him they were just something through which one had to go in order to get to the important stuff: the practical workshops. He chuckled at Trito and his concerns. He had seen it before. He thought to himself, "It is such a shame that all that passion and concern can't be focused on doing something, rather than on this artsy visionary stuff. Such a waste of time and energy."

The workshops did not disappoint Zadok. The people who led them were highly competent in terms of their experience, their knowledge, and their ability to communicate. The only difficulty for Zadok was choosing which ones to attend. And it was his choice. Yahweh had instructed both Zadok and Trito to attend these sessions together. To Zadok's credit, he invited Trito to select some he would enjoy, but Trito was so disgusted that he left it all to Zadok. All through the workshops, Zadok kept muttering, "I wish I had known this." Or, "Imagine how that could have made a difference." Or simply, "Wow!"

Zadok's being awed by these presentations was astounding, considering his own accomplishments. After the exiles returned from Babylon, Jerusalem was in such disrepair that few could imagine how to restore it to even a glimpse of its former glory. Zadok and his followers accomplished the inconceivable. Many of his day thought it was a miracle. As they watched Jerusalem's rubble rise up, as they experienced a nation coming together and functioning again, almost everyone grew to trust Zadok and his management plan. The proof was in the pudding, and Zadok and his people were putting Jerusalem back together again.

Almost everyone was impressed—but not all. Trito and his followers watched as their broad vision of faithfulness, received and confirmed in the empty forsakenness of Babylon, was silenced and dismissed. Now, during the workshops at the "From Rubble to Renewal" conference, Trito, like a reluctant disciple, silently shadowed Zadok through the workshops. Zadok attended a workshop on how to make facilities more hospitable and user-friendly. This included how to make them fit into the culture and become acceptable. Thinking of his struggle with the Persians in the past, Zadok commented to Trito as they left the workshop, "I wish I had known that. Instead of calling it a Jewish Temple, it would have saved a lot of confusion if we had called it a Community Temple. After all, as they said, it doesn't really change anything important; it's just a name." Trito almost fainted.

The workshop on worship might have attracted Trito if it had been entitled anything but "Demystifying Praise: Worship as Meeting People's Needs." When they attended the hour-long pep rally where it was mentioned, "Sometimes you have to not mention God too much, because it can offend people who have been disappointed with God in the past," Zadok was wired. "If only our priests had known this stuff. This upbeat, optimistic, inspirational, and relevant worship would have drawn back in droves a profoundly disappointed people." Trito wanted to gag.

Trito thought it couldn't get more frustrating, but it did. The workshop "Securing Membership Loyalty" was packed. Trito thought it was ironic that they ran out of their four-color handouts. As he handed his to those around him, he said, "I can share with my friend." Zadok was engaged in this workshop like no other. As they were waiting for it to get started, Zadok told Trito, "This was our biggest challenge: how to get people to be loyal Jews again. We knew it was key to the whole project of rebuilding our nation." Then the workshop started. It was being led by the customer-service specialists from a major theme park. They told their story of how they created a place where people came back again and again and again. People stood in lines to participate. They traveled from great distances. And they said boldly, "The same can be true for you. It is not magic (although magic was in the title of one of their main attractions); it is common sense applied with discipline." The rest of the hour was the sharing of these common-sense practices and principles. For Trito, what made absurd what was already appalling was that the presentation was done by people dressed as cartoon characters from the theme park. Each principle was identified with a character who made the presentation. Zadok was impressed and left the workshop whistling some catchy tune that had been background music to the presentations. Trito prayed that God might quickly haul him back to Babylon. It is a small world, after all.

For Zadok, the workshop day went by all too fast. For Trito, it was like experiencing adolescence all over again in six short hours of pure anguish. They attended three other workshops. One was on leadership styles; it talked a lot about vision, but it seemed to Trito that the vision was not the leader's, but was the result of the latest surveys. The importance and necessity of verifiable targets was also asserted: goals, objectives, targets for every project, and every dimension of ministry. The task of the leader is to keep people on track, the workshop asserted. Trito, remembering his time in Babylon, wondered to himself what would happen if God sent a surprise, changed the agenda, maybe called forth a foreigner, like Cyrus, to be his agent of change. How do you plan for surprises?

There was another workshop on the program church and how you must be continually developing new programs to meet new needs, because the world is changing so fast. The homogeneous principle provided the key to making programs work: design programs so that people gather with people who have similar needs, dreams, life circumstances, or whatever. Keep diversity to a minimum. Programs should be a sanctuary from a world full of increasing pluralism, much of which a person cannot dismiss but must simply endure. Trito remembered God's vision of all nations, all people, all differences, being joined together in God's kingdom. This radical vision of hope portrayed a gracious community of strangers becoming one.

The last workshop they attended was about justice issues. The leader told them it was important to get involved in justice issues. However, he said, you must focus on charity—local charity. When you get involved in wider societal issues, you cause conflict. Conflict in a church is not a good thing. Find one or two "safe" things to do, and then make a big deal out of it. "People want to feel good about helping, but they really are not interested in being change agents," was the line both Zadok and Trito remembered. "Makes good practical sense," Zadok proclaimed. Trito just shook his head in despair.

The long ride home was quiet and uneventful for the most part. Zadok had packets of information and handouts organized neatly into file folders. Like an engineer planning to design and build a new structure, Zadok was carefully planning, step by step, how to proceed. At first Zadok was so excited he forgot who he was traveling with and shared a few ideas, looking for some feedback. However, after either no response or some not-so-subtle gestures of disgust, Zadok muttered quietly to himself or not at all.

Zadok was concerned about God's people and the sorry state in which they found themselves at the beginning of the twenty-first century. Something needed to be done. The thought of tackling such a big project and managing an efficient and effective response brought him great joy and satisfaction. Trito looked out the window at the landscape. Most of the time he wondered which way he was going. Was he returning from Babylon or was he being taken captive back into exile? Finally, in deep despair, he realized it likely made no difference. The level of anxiety and fear he felt at "Rubble to Renewal Conference" would likely win the day. In the face of such angst, the fix-it mentality of Zadok and his ilk would be so attractive. Trito knew from experience that vision would be held captive and silent.

As they drew closer to home, Trito prayed over and over again for the ability to persevere and trust the vision, even when it was humiliated and forgotten by others. He recommitted himself to being bold in his witness to God's expansive and transformative passion to not just fix the world, but to redeem it and to bring forth a new reality, a new way of being. "Give me strength to surrender to this vision, to this passion, to this God." This was the prayer Trito prayed. And then he added, "For the sake of all creation, let it be so."

Upon their return, they reported to Yahweh about their adventure. Each was honest and persuasive. Each tried not to be overcritical of the other, but their differences could not be denied. God's deep desire to reunite these two ancient foes had failed again.

In short order, and with more than a little frustration, God proclaimed, "It is my mission to bring healing and wholeness, shalom, to my creation. It will not happen when my own witnesses cannot find healing with each other. Go. And I will wait. For one day shalom, even for you two, will happen."

Zadok walked out and immediately began talking about a program to make shalom a reality. If he could rebuild Jerusalem, he could fix this problem as well.

Trito walked out and renewed his conviction never to forget the vision of shalom. Somebody, in this noisy world of pragmatism and technique, must hold on to the vision.

And God waited, and still waits.

PART TWO

FIRST STEPS BEYOND CHURCH GROWTH

One of my favorite Bill Cosby routines involves a football coach giving a half-time pep talk. Cosby, the coach, stirs the team up to a fevered frenzy. They are screaming, pounding on lockers, grunting, and ready to win the world. At the peak of their exuberance, the coach says, "Okay, men, go get 'em." Then there is a dead silence; the door out of the locker room is locked tight.

Imagining the shape of congregations in a postmodern age can be like getting fired up for the second half of a football game. As essential as imagination is, we also must find a way to open the door. Looking ahead, the excitement of moving beyond church growth can stir the hearts and imagination of the church. Looking back, we can find ample reason to honor the past and its gifts and yet know we must commit ourselves to moving ahead. But finally, looking ahead and looking back is not enough; we must open the door and take the first steps.

Shaped by modernity, more often than not I become immobilized when I finally have to make a decision and move ahead. My children laugh at me when we go to the video store. I am traumatized by the experience. In the face of all the possible video choices, I want to make sure I don't make a mistake. After much too much deliberation, my children plead with me to pick one, any one. They heap scorn on me by saying that if we don't decide soon, we will have spent all our time looking for a movie rather than watching one.

If the church is to move beyond church growth, it must choose some first steps. Taking the first steps into this new way of being church is more important than figuring out exactly what those steps might be. We must let go of the idea that there is one right choice and instead be bold and risk venturing forth.

Below are some imaginative first steps. They are not by any means the only steps one could or should take. These steps may or may not lead to the desired results. From the present vantage point, they seem promising and worth taking. I pray, even if they lead to a dead end, that the journey will be filled with learning and will prod further exploration. Maybe these first steps will instill new imagination about another more promising and effective direction.

The first steps highlighted in the following chapters begin with the congregation. Part Three continues with some tentative proposals for pastoral and other set-apart leaders. A postmodern world needs congregations set apart to bear witness to God's reign in Jesus Christ. The mission field stands before us, and "the fields are ripe for the harvest." However, very few, if any, organizations grow past their leaders. Any first steps to move beyond church growth, therefore, must involve both the congregation and the pastoral leader. To focus on one to the exclusion of the other leads to getting all fired up to engage in the mission, only to find the door locked shut.

The time has come to open the door and take the first steps. Let us go forth in the name of Christ; and taking some first steps, let us risk moving beyond church growth and entering into the adventure God has in store for us.

3

A CONGREGATIONAL FAITH AUDIT

A congregation wrestling with the vision of the "triadic notion of faithful community" (praise, righteousness, and compassion) recently asked what kind of benchmarks there might be for their ministry. How might they evaluate their ministry? What kind of questions would help discern their being faithful? To ask it another way, is it possible to develop a congregational faith audit?

Modernity evaluates almost all of life numerically and statistically. Thus, in most contemporary congregations, the benchmarks for faithful ministry are membership numbers, worship attendance, and financial reports. Sometimes congregations evaluate their success and failure based on the size of their facility, the number of paid staff, or the extensiveness of their programmatic offerings.

All these criteria focus on the modern fascination with *doing*. They stress the institutional nature of the church, a mechanistic view, and foster a management model of ministry. Modern evaluation tools encourage a consumeristic notion of ministry in which the meeting of people's needs is equated with faithfulness. Ministry is faithful when it is successful; it is successful when people respond in a way that their response can be measured. This makes it possible to keep score.

This dominant view of ministry is evident both in the informal conversation of both pastoral and lay congregational leaders, as well as in the formal ways in which ministry is evaluated. Congregational and denominational statistical reports, and evaluations based on the productivity of leaders, are but two indicators of the modern science of keeping score and the fascination with growth. And growth is always quantifiable.

There are a number of problems with the modern approach to congregational evaluation. First of all, a solely quantifiable approach to faithful community is not supported biblically. Growth—numerical growth—is not a dominant biblical theme. Douglas John Hall notes that the only place Jesus speaks about this kind of growth is in the parable of building bigger barns: fascination with growth, then, is negative. It is true that when Peter preaches at Pentecost, three thousand are baptized: thanks be to God! Yet it is also true that, when Stephen preaches, he is stoned to death: thanks be to God! Proclaiming the gospel, no matter what the response is, is common to both stories. A professor once said, "Preach the gospel and get out of the way." The proclamation of the Word of God has validity, no matter what the response. The primary task of the church involves proclaiming God's Word, not focusing on the results.

Second, a statistical approach to congregational evaluation inevitably focuses on *doing* and not on *being*. It drives the congregation back on itself. Such self-preoccupation refocuses the vision away from God, leading to discouragement and despair. Because the focus is on the congregation, the pastor, congregational leaders, programming, or the needs of others, the congregation becomes disconnected from the sole source of life and hope: Jesus. The modern agenda in which God is no longer necessary finally wins the day. No wonder congregations feel so empty!

A significant challenge for those called to imagine faithful ministry in a postmodern age is to discern benchmarks for faithful congregational witness. What might a "Congregational Faith Audit" look like for Glimpse of God Church, a congregation that seeks to bear witness to the reign of God in all they do for the sake of the world?

The following is an initial response to this question.

The Audit

Listed below are a number of questions under each of three categories. The questions emerge out of two visions of faithful congregational life.

First, the three categories reflect the triadic notion of faithful community. Congregations are faithful when they live the dynamic tension between praise, righteousness, and compassion. Praise acknowledges that God, revealed in Jesus Christ, is the sole source of life and hope for the future. Righteousness claims that a faithful community orders and structures the life it receives as a gift by being in a right relationship with the One who calls it into being. Compassion announces that the stranger, the outsider, the voiceless, the poor, and the enemy are welcome into the heart of the community of faith and received as gifts from God. The "Congregational Faith Audit" evaluates the congregation in light of how they are upholding the tension between these three dynamics.

Second, the questions under each of the three categories stem from a picture of faithful community in the early church. Justin Martyr's first-century portrayal of the practice of the gathered believers provides the content of the questions. Justin Martyr's description is as follows:

> On Sunday, all are gathered together in unity. The records of the apostles or the writings of the prophets are read as long as time allows. The presider exhorts and invites us into the pattern of these good things. Then we all stand and offer prayer.
>
> When we have concluded the prayer, bread is set out together with wine. . . . The presider then offers prayer and thanksgiving and the people sing out their assent, saying the "Amen." There is distribution of the things over which thanks has been said and each person participates, and these things are sent to those who are not present.
>
> Those who are prosperous give what they wish according to each one's own choice, and the collection is deposited with the presider, who aids orphans and widows, those in want because of disease, those in prison, and foreigners who are staying here.

> We hold this meeting together on Sunday since it is the first
> day, on which God, having transformed darkness and matter, cre-
> ated the world. On the same day Jesus Christ our Savior rose from
> the dead. On Sunday he appeared to his apostles and disciples and
> taught them these things which we present to you.[1]

Consider the life of the congregation in light of these questions:

Praise

*1. How often does the congregation gather? What is the character of
the congregation's gathering?*

God's people gather. Christian faith is communal. You cannot
be Christian alone. Gatherings take place in a variety of settings:
worship, education, fellowship, administration, and so forth. How
often a congregation gathers as a community and the shape of that
gathering is an indicator of faithfulness. What is the vision that this
community gathers around? Is it clearly articulated and embraced?
What are the symbols that call this community together? (Holy
Scripture or the church constitution? Bible or bank account?) The
vision and symbols around which a community gather reveal the
character of the community.

*2. What is the congregation's meal life like? Is the meal life known
by the smell of bread and wine? What stories are told around the
table? What is the nature of the conversation as the people gather
around the table of Holy Communion?*

The body of Christ feasts upon and is nourished by the body
and blood of Jesus, the crucified and risen Lord. The smell of
bread and wine is the aroma that identifies the community and
their mission. The community's table manners and the frequency
of their gathering around the meal are a means by which the congregation forms and can assess its identity. Meal stories, the
preaching of the Word, reveal whose table is set, why the meal is
served, and the nature of the hospitality that is offered.

Righteousness

1. What is the nature of biblical teaching and reflection in the congregation?

A faithful community seeks to live out its life based on the biblical story. The extent to which Bible stories and biblical language are used when the community gathers indicates where the congregation is rooted. Because these biblical stories are not the dominant cultural stories that compel our attention, a primary task of the congregation becomes teaching the Bible as a story language (a grammar) that gives meaning to life. Like all foreign languages, when people neglect using the language, they lose their capacity for fluency, and the language loses its power to shape their character. What language does the congregation speak as its primary language? Language is what orders and structures our lives.

2. How essential is our visitation (with bread and wine in our hands and their smell on our breath) to those of the congregation who are in need?

One of the characteristics of a faithful community is care for members of the congregation. But the care provided is not a matter of personal niceness and civility. Justin Martyr's portrait of a faithful community reveals that visitation involves bringing bread and wine (or at least their aroma) to those who are absent from the community. To say it another way, visitation to those in need is for the express purpose of providing care by announcing the presence of Jesus and his kingdom promise. Implied in this concept of visitation is that the language spoken reflects the language spoken by the community when it gathers around its meal. In this sense, visitation is as much about evangelical witness as it is about care.

Compassion

1. What is the nature of our congregational and individual prayer life? Who do we invite into our community through prayer?

Prayer is central to the life of the faithful community. That prayer is practiced, and practiced often, indicates the faithfulness of the congregation. But a more careful assessment must be made. The cliché is true: Be careful what you pray for; God may answer. What a congregation prays for indicates to whom it listens, who has its ears. People, events, and issues are invited into the very core of a congregation through its prayer life. What is more, the congregation connects with the world through its prayers. Thomas Merton claims that radical prayer drives us into the world.

2. What is the nature of our offerings to orphans, widows, strangers: briefly, to all who are in need?

Justin Martyr concludes his description of the gathering of early Christians by speaking of sacrificial, gracious, benevolent giving. The congregation is invited to give itself away not just spiritually, but in terms of the practical, everyday components of life: money, time, and resources. Stewardship reflects the trust and faith of a community. Such stewardship implies individual members giving to the congregation, and also the congregation giving to those outside. Justin Martyr's picture reveals trust, almost blind trust, in the "president." When offerings are made, people lose control. In contemporary congregational life, financial giving (not the only kind of stewardship, but a facet of stewardship in our day that must not be denied) to those outside the control of the congregation is an act of faith. How does the congregation give itself away without having to be in control of the results?

∽

Imagine receiving such a "Congregational Faith Audit" annually from jurisdictional offices. Would these questions provide benchmarks to assist in an honest assessment of congregational faithfulness?

4

DEPROGRAMMING THE CHURCH

A mother and father wait, in pain. Their precious daughter has run away. Once, in a childish fit of rage, she might have hidden in the garage with a pillow, a favorite blanket, and a tattered teddy bear. But this time their daughter, a young woman, has fled her world and been embraced by another. She has joined a new group and welcomed a new life. Her parents call it a cult.

Now they wait, they pray, and they plan. They wait and wonder what drove their daughter to this other world. The experts say that profound disappointment caused their daughter's betrayal. Was the disappointment with her parents and family? Her peer group? Or was it the specific societal setting in which she lived? Was it a deep discontent with her world and the direction her life, at its most basic level, was heading? The parents expect no answers to these questions. They only know that their beloved child found her life so empty that she fled to a completely separate way of life. Was she seduced? Yes. Did she go willingly? Yes. Will she ever return? Maybe. Will her parents' life ever be the same again? No. The parents wait with these questions.

They wait and hold each other. They have read that this kind of trauma can divide and destroy a marriage and a family. Friends encourage them to focus on who they are and on their love for each other. Their ability to discern and claim the core foundation of their life together will be the key to surviving these difficult and humiliating days of self-doubt and fear. Attending to their life together will be essential if their daughter returns.

As they wait, they also pray for their daughter to return. They long for her to come home. They hope that their "little girl" will recall who she is and whose she is. They cry out persistently for her to know that their door is open. They pray that she knows they wait like the father in the parable of the prodigal son, the father who graciously receives the wayward child.

As they wait and pray, they also plan. If their daughter returns—when she returns—what will they do? How will they respond? The task, they are told by the experts, will be to deprogram her. But, as tempting as it may be, they cannot deprogram their daughter. They are the ones who must be deprogrammed. To reintegrate their daughter back into their love, to move her through and beyond her profound disappointment, will take patience, time, and most of all, trust. Her restoration is not a matter of focusing on changing her, but rather on their being transformed so that they can be open.

The parents must trust that healing will happen through their persistent presence. They must be deeply rooted and calm, and they must not fall prey to the powerful pressure to "fix" their daughter. They must provide a sanctuary that is at once profoundly open to their daughter's disappointment and anger and firmly founded in an identity that cannot be shaken. They must learn to live in radical, vulnerable hospitality.

With this in mind, the parents plan for their daughter's return by attending to themselves and grounding themselves in who they are and what they believe. Through this confidence in who and whose they are, they can begin to be open and even learn from their daughter's betrayal. They continually struggle to trust what has shaped them and will shape them so that they can truly attend to and be present with their daughter. And maybe, just maybe, they can foster new trust, so that one day they can be present with their daughter in her deepest disappointments.

The struggle is to trust. Over and over again they become afraid and anxious, and start to provide answers instead of living in the painful questions. They move from preparing to be hospitably present to providing a fix for whatever problem or disruption is experienced. At its core, the problem is a pervasive disappointment in an existence filled with emptiness and despair instead of meaning and purpose. The hurt revealed in this emptiness drives the instinctive need to fill it, fix the despair, and somehow become optimistic. The parents deprogram themselves, preparing to receive their daughter by practicing the discipline of not rushing to the quick fix, but instead learning to trust their presence and the transformation such a presence will conceive.

Be clear: they do not wait passively. The parents actively anticipate and continually live as if on tiptoes. This is no quiet, contemplative prayer life, isolated from the world. Their prayers are cries of lament and focus on the realities of the world, the real world, in which they and their beloved daughter, wherever she may be, are engaged. Their preparation is no academic, dispassionate, intellectual exercise. Their preparation demands a repentance, conversion, and venture into faith that will transform them forever, even as it grounds their identity more deeply.

༄

This parable is one way to describe the present experience of the church. North American society and its inhabitants, most of whom once considered themselves members of the household of the church, are now like the daughter who has run away from her identity. Disappointment with failed promises—in the church, to be sure, but also in the totality of life—have driven them to other answers, other fixes. They have joined other cults; or we might say that they have accommodated to the dominant culture, which ever more reveals itself as alien to the gospel vision. The beloved have betrayed their identity and have turned away from their home, the church. In search of meaning, the beloved run away from their church home and seek out answers and hope in places outside the church's understanding of meaning and life.

The church, like parents of a child who has betrayed them and cut herself off from them, must now wait, pray, and trust. The temptation is for the church to aggressively pursue what has been lost, recapture it, and then force it to return. In psychological terms, this overfunctioning builds a barrier through which it becomes impossible for the lost one to return, even when that is their desire. The church's love for the world fuels this destructive behavior that results in the opposite of what is intended. This is not just a result of zealous imperialistic motives or longing for increased market share; it is a deep, heartfelt passion to recover what is lost. However, such pursuit, no matter how well meant, is the opposite of waiting. The church must actively wait, paying careful attention to the world and listening for any word about the beloved. The church waits and wonders, and thus, ironically, makes itself open for a welcomed return. But the church must deprogram itself of the need to crusade for the lost and drive them back home. In such a pursuit, the church drives the lost away and, more often than not, loses its own sense of identity. Like parents who will do anything for their child, and by doing so, forget to be parents, the church must wait and trust that being the church is what the lost ones need. When the church loses this sense of faithful waiting, active waiting, and becomes lost in its own pursuit, the church finds itself accommodating to the very culture it has previously seen as the problem.

The church also prays. The prayers that rise from the church are filled with lament, loss, grief, and deep longing for the restoration of all that is now broken. These prayers are not just for the return of the beloved. The prayers are also for all those who are lost, that they may be safe and kept secure in the love of a God who promises to be with them, even if they are not aware of this promise. Prayer, in this sense, is more than just a reciting of words. Prayer becomes a way of thinking, engaging feelings, and demanding God's action. Prayer is a posture, a way of being. The call is not just to *do* prayers, but to *be* a people of prayer.

Prayer acknowledges dependence on God, not on oneself. As someone said, "It is not so important what you pray, but that you pray." This kind of prayer profoundly shapes the character and actions of both individuals and congregations. When prayer becomes a posture, a way of being, congregations can set aside the hyperactivity of always having the answer, the fix, the responsibility. Instead of focusing on itself and its duties, the congregation surrenders this to God in prayer and paradoxically has room for the questions and brokenness it wishes to address.

Finally, the church trusts that all it needs to be is its particular presence in the world. The church's complete mission is to be an actively waiting and praying people whose identity is rooted in God's story of redemption through Jesus Christ. The church prepares for the return of those who left and commits itself to not falling prey to "fixing" those who have gone astray. Vulnerable hospitality becomes the practice the church refines, because it is a community marked by trust in God. To say it another way, the church is a faithful people, full of faith and thus called to live in uncertainty.

Entering this parable challenges the church to deprogram itself, not the one who has left and entered another cult. In order to be an evangelical community, the church must realize that God has provided them with all they need. The church must let go of the programs used to imperialistically reintegrate people. Lusting after quick fixes, attending workshops on how to grow and bring the lost home, learning more and more techniques to be relevant and exciting, are all finally counterproductive. These programmatic products are a part of the disappointment that drove the world away from the church in the first place. More often than not, the products offered serve a purpose more closely aligned with some ideological preference or personal conviction than with God's will, and thus they inevitably ended in ever-increasing disillusionment. This is the history of Christendom since Constantine. Although even today the church may experience some initial successes, most likely the disappointment will only surface again, and the leave-taking from the church will only be more traumatic and lasting. Instead, the church must wait, continually centered in its story and its attentiveness to the world. It must continue to attend to itself and its core foundations. This is done primarily through worship and liturgy. For it is in worship and liturgy, which redirect the congregation's attention to God and neighbor, that the church is most authentically itself and thus most profoundly open.

As counterintuitive as it may feel, the church must deprogram itself, and learn to *be*—not do, but be—a community that waits by attending to itself, enters the world through prayer, and prepares for the return of the beloved by learning radical, gracious hospitality.

Once, while involved in an immersion experience, I was visiting a homeless shelter for youth in a small city in the southwestern United States. We were encouraged to eat with the youth, help in serving them lunch, and talk with them. As the meal began, a middle-aged man dressed in a suit came in and sat down at a table. No one said anything. It was clear the folks who ran the site knew the man. He sat at a table with a number of kids, talked, and ate. At the end of meal, he put on an apron and helped clear the tables. It was then that I talked with him.

He told me he was a sales representative for a company, and he traveled through these southwestern states. He also told me that he had a fifteen-year-old daughter who had run away. He did not know where she was or what was happening to her. As we put chairs up on the table, he said that at first he looked and looked for her, but finally he realized he could not fix the problem. Now what he did was pray for her. He also called home to his wife twice a day, and he never was away from home more than three days in a row. Each time he called, each time he opened the door to his house, he expected to hear the sound of his daughter's voice. He would not allow the expectation to be dashed by his continual disappointment. And, he told me, almost every noon, in whatever city he finds himself, he eats at a homeless shelter and talks with kids who have run away. He does not tell them to go home, or how wrong it is to leave, or how much their parents hurt and ache for their return. He just loves them and listens.

As the man prepared to leave the shelter, he looked at me and said, "I do this in part because I hope someone else has just finished eating with my daughter and letting her know she is loved. Maybe if she finally can know she is loved, she will come home."

This "deprogrammed" father provides a model for a "deprogrammed" church in a postmodern age. The father reminds the church to wait expectantly. To pray fervently. And to learn radical, gracious hospitality.

5

RECLAIMING THE SABBATH: ONE TEXT AT A TIME

Beth pounded the steering wheel as the light changed and she was forced to stop at yet another intersection. She was late for the meeting at church, and it was her doctor's fault. As Beth fumed, she realized her frustration with her doctor was not only about making her late. She was not pleased with how he had responded to her request.

Beth's appointment was occasioned by her ever-increasing fatigue and grumpiness. She just did not feel like herself. She easily got defensive and short with others. Life was no longer fun. She was convinced that there was something physically wrong with her. More than that, she was sure there was some drug, some pill that could fix her and restore her health. She wanted her doctor to make her well. She assumed it would be no problem. After all, what else was a doctor for?

She soon found out how wrong she was. The doctor took her complaints seriously, but he did not respond with a pill and a quick fix. The doctor spent a long time asking all kinds of questions about her life, her eating habits, her work, and her family. He also talked with her about the aging process, a conversation that did not sit well with her. What she expected to be a short visit ending with a prescription became a physical and a lecture. The doctor told her he was not interested in masking the real problem with a pill. Over and over she was told to take a holistic view of what was happening. She left the doctor's office with another appointment scheduled and an assignment. The doctor told her to spend some time picturing what she longed for her life to become and then considering at least one way she could make that picture a reality.

Pulling into the church parking lot, she was still upset. All she wanted was a quick fix, a few pills. What she got instead was an invitation to a lifestyle change. Beth muttered to herself, "Some doctor. Why is he making me jump through hoops instead of helping me? If they are smart enough to put a man on the moon, why can't they fix my problem? What am I paying him for?"

Beth chaired the Renewal Taskforce at church. Their mission involved planning and implementing a renewal program for the congregation. What was once, at least in their memories, a vital and vibrant ministry had become sluggish and fatigued. Congregation members had started to get grumpy and irritable with each other and even with God. Finally, they decided it was time to fix the problem and make things right again. Of course, this demanded establishing a taskforce and crafting a plan.

This was the second meeting of the group. Last week they had discussed the problems. Each member of the taskforce committed to returning with something he or she could do to fix one of the problems. Beth assumed that tonight they would prioritize these fixes and begin to make plans for implementation. It should be as easy as that.

For the second time in one day, she was dead wrong. People took the assignment seriously, and each of the seven people on the committee came with a solution to a problem. However, it was clear before long that each was invested in his or her particular fix. Everyone was sure he or she had the perfect way to correct the problem. As Beth listened and tried to foster some consensus, the scene began to feel vaguely familiar. The level of frustration in the room rose higher and higher; finally, someone pounded a fist on the table and said, "Look. What we need is a program we can implement quickly that will make us right again. Let's pick a program, any program, and get started."

The words that came out of Beth's mouth surprised even her. "I don't think it will be helpful if we mask our problems with a program. Our inability to be excited about any particular direction only confirms this. Let's try another approach." She couldn't believe she was going to do this—but she did. "Here's our assignment. Each of us will go home and picture what we believe God wants this congregation to become. Pray about it. Then come back with at least one picture that might become a reality."

She could tell the whole committee felt as uneasy as she had been in the doctor's office. Yet, either because of their frustration or because of her suggestion's inherent wisdom, they agreed to her approach.

That is how it all began. In a few months, the congregation was continually invited to experience renewal "One Text at a Time." This was not a program to be taken like a pill, but a pilgrimage to which they were called to surrender. It was not a strategy full of goals and objectives, measurable results, and the like. Rather, they were called to venture forth and allow the texts to have their way with the congregation. The outcome they hoped for was not to mask the problem with a quick fix, but to reorder their life together so they might name honestly those things that inhibit life. Beth found herself saying over and over again, "It's a lifestyle thing."

The pastor, who sat on the taskforce but had remained quiet during the proceedings, provided the initial focus for living "One Text at a Time." The pastor was encouraged to preach, teach, and use, almost exclusively, the language of the text for the coming week. Whether it was devotions before meetings, the opening prayer for confirmation class, or home visitations, the pastor challenged herself to see her ministry "One Text at a Time." To make this happen more effectively, she committed herself to memorizing the gospel text for each week. Often, she also memorized the appointed prayer of the day. Each week she imagined she was entering a new country that spoke a different language—the language of the appointed text. As she made her pilgrimage through the week, she was continually amazed at what she saw when she viewed life through the lens of the text. When there were funerals or weddings, she would preach on the text in which she was living. "One Text at a Time" simplified her ministry, and at the same time brought a depth of meaning and understanding she had not known before. "One Text at a Time" brought new joy to her vocation as a pastoral leader.

One of the other first steps the taskforce took was to establish one benchmark they could measure. They would try to track one statistic: not worship attendance, or membership numbers, or the amount of the offering. They wanted to increase the percentage of people who attended worship after having wrestled with the text before they arrived on Sunday morning.

Soon there were a number of gatherings each week for the study of the texts for the coming Sunday. They were called "Word for the Week." One, for young adults, was at a coffee shop in the late afternoon. Another was for high school students and was held early in the morning before school. A couple of others were scattered throughout the week. Whenever and wherever people wanted to gather around the texts, it became a top priority.

Realizing that a greater number of people were coming to worship informed by the text demanded more careful attention to worship planning. Now people noticed the connections between the liturgical words, hymns, actions, the environment, and the texts that occasioned the gathering. Assisting ministers began praying the texts, and the prayers were heard by many as being rooted not just in the congregation's deep desires, but also in God's Word of promise and hope. The more people were informed by the text, the more difficult preaching became for the pastor. "One Text at a Time" provoked renewed commitment to worship and preaching.

A lectionary-based Sunday school curriculum had been used for years, but "One Text at a Time" focused new energy on this ministry. Teachers felt like what they were teaching was key to the ongoing life of the congregation, as well as to the children. Parents found children, even young children, more engaged in worship. In addition to Sunday morning, a weekly after-school ministry for elementary children dealing with worship, music, and the arts structured itself around "One Text at a Time."

The taskforce kept meeting and wondering how they could embrace "One Text at a Time" even more fully. At one of their meetings, one of the members spoke of having lunch with a coworker who attended the congregation. The coworker was just catching on to this "One Text at a Time" practice. What most amazed the coworker was how honest he felt living this way. It was not a system, although there was some order. There was no expected outcome. One week's text sometimes even contradicted the previous week's text. The process was not neat; it was not a paint-by-numbers approach. Living "One Text at a Time" was messy. He said, "Engaging life 'One Text at a Time' is true to life. Life is not a machine, but a messy set of realities through which we must find our way. In order to muck through this mess, every-one needs some way to find a direction. 'One Text at a Time' is a gift the church has given me. It is a gift of great integrity."

As the taskforce member spoke, they realized how their initial charge to renew the congregation had now grown into an evan-gelical mission that addressed not only the congregation, but all of life. Beth thought to herself, "'One Text at a Time' is becoming a lifestyle."

A young couple at church had just adopted two children from a Ukraine orphanage. One day they asked the pastor about how they might begin to do family devotions. This simple question led to yet another "One Text at a Time" exploration. Soon, the weekly bulletin and the monthly newsletter provided the weekly readings, along with the Prayer of the Day. In addition, there were daily texts that related to the weekly texts.[1] Now, in households throughout the congregation, people were gathering around these texts in their personal and family devotions.

The congregation continues to discover more and more ways to live "One Text at a Time." A group of people committed to intercessory prayer is beginning to gather. They pray for people, the congregation, and the world, but they pray through the texts for the coming week. The texts give their voices integrity and authenticity. Their text-informed prayers have become a significant source of renewal for the congregation.

Presently, a group is gathering to consider how to integrate new members into the congregation. What they seek to do is not to focus on getting people connected to other people for its own sake. Rather, they desire to challenge those who seek to be part of this ministry to get connected "One Text at a Time." They are trying to find every possible way a person can get connected to the text each week. They want to invite new members to choose one place, in addition to Sunday worship, to get connected to the text. They are confident this will provide a way to integrate new members into a community lifestyle—a "One Text at a Time" lifestyle.

At an annual meeting, someone raised his hand with a question about the budget. He noticed the budget line for Conferences and Workshops was not being used. There was also a budget line for the Congregational Renewal Taskforce that was really underspent. He found this interesting and wondered why it was the case.

Beth stood up to respond. She spoke of how they used to attend one glitzy church-renewal seminar after another. Each promised their congregation would be successful and grow. Each seminar had a variety of programs that it promoted. Each said it was the perfect remedy for a particular problem. But rarely did attending these workshops and committing to these programs make any difference. So, she said, "We have quit attending quick-fix workshops."

She was quiet for a minute, then she looked at the congregation and said, "Programs are like pills; they are expensive and usually only mask the disease. We as a taskforce decided to abandon this pharmaceutical approach to renewal and to commit to a lifestyle change. We found out that God has already given us all we need: God's Holy Word, a community open to wrestling with that Word, the presence of the Holy Spirit to open eyes and hearts, and a commitment to worship and stand under the lordship of a God who is revealed in the Word made flesh, Jesus. All of that is a free gift. On the one hand, it is the least expensive thing we can imagine. That is why the budget line is not spent. On the other hand, as we embrace living 'One Text at A Time,' we will find it will demand a lifestyle change. I must warn you: watch out; this lifestyle is costly in a whole different way."

Beth returned many times to her doctor in the coming years. Each time she wished he had some magic pill that would fix her body and spirit. Each time he challenged her to envision her life more holistically. There were times she was tempted to grasp at one of the many pharmaceutical answers to her life's questions. But each time, she would remember what was happening at church. She would recall the renewal experienced by a congregation committing itself to a lifestyle, not a program: a congregation that lived "One Text at Time."

6

DRAWING THE LINE:
REFLECTIONS ON CHURCH GROWTH
AND WORSHIP

The conversation took place at a pastors meeting and lasted only a few minutes. Paul, a neighboring pastor, had been sharing his passion for a new mission congregation. I was impressed by his commitment and zeal for gospel witness. He shared his conviction for the spreading of the good news of Jesus and the need for a congregation on the west side of town. A group of lay leaders and pastors were about to begin raising money from local congregations so the mission could become a reality. Paul wanted my support and my commitment to embrace the mission and help ensure its success.

I asked about the character of the congregation and its leadership. His response confirmed the rumor I had been hearing. When the conversation ended, we were both troubled. Paul was troubled because I had told him I could not support the mission.

I could not support the new mission, because it would be developed using basic church-growth principles. When I shared my unwillingness to join in this endeavor, Paul responded with disbelief and then asked the hard question that has troubled me since he asked it. "Is that enough of a reason to not support the spreading of the gospel of Jesus Christ?" Paul did not ask this question in a mean-spirited way or to shame me. He was sincerely perplexed and bewildered by my response.

I feel I owe Paul a response to his provocative and profound question. Here it is.

Paul, thank you for your passion and commitment to spread the gospel of Jesus Christ. Your willingness to champion a mission congregation in the community reveals that commitment.

Thank you for your deep desire to engage other congregations and pastors in this mission endeavor. I appreciate the conversation we had the other day. I appreciate your openness to my concerns and your great gift of not becoming defensive in light of my lack of support for the project.

Most of all, thank you for the question you asked. You seem to have a gift for asking good questions. When I shared that I could not support the new mission because it will be organized around church-growth principles, you responded with a question I feel I must answer. I write this as much for myself as for you. You asked me, "Is your conviction about church growth enough of a reason to not support the spreading of the gospel of Jesus Christ?" I understood you to be asking, "Why do you draw the line here? Why are the methods of church growth so problematic for you?"

When we talked, our discussion about church growth quickly turned toward issues about worship. Your response to my concern about church growth focused on worship styles. Worship provides a great door into the conversation. However, for me, the style of worship is not of principal concern. Worship styles are symptoms of deeper issues. The underlying assumptions used when choosing worship styles are the focus of my concern.

Devoting attention to worship makes good sense because congregational character is shaped by worship. The way a congregation gathers, prays, hears God's Word proclaimed, sings, and shares in a holy meal and a sacred washing determines who they are and how they will live out their life together. Worship crafts the congregation's character by inviting the community of faith to surrender itself to God. The act of worship is an act of surrender. Individuals lose themselves to the community. The community as a whole also relinquishes itself to the God who has called them into being, redeemed them, and fills them with the Holy Spirit.

Here is where I draw the line. Congregations whose worship life focuses on meeting people's needs, providing entertaining or inspiring experiences, or affirming the contemporary condition of the individual by presenting a relevant and useful God, crosses the line for me. When worship attends primarily to the individual, it is no longer Christian worship. A community that gathers as a helping institution might provide some effective tools for living and may be of great service to the community. However, the character of such a community is little different than a service club.

Inevitably, worship then becomes a tool for marketing and for serving the needs of individuals. Surveying the needs of the target market, communicating effectively based on the target market's perceived needs, packaging the product so the individual will embrace it, and building loyalty become key practices. When a congregation's worship life stresses these components, the gospel of Jesus Christ becomes just another commodity. This inevitably results in living the unquestioned creed of today's society, "The customer comes first." As is so evident in our self-indulgent culture, when people's wants are the focus, they cannot see their essential needs.

Here I must make my stand. My convictions demand supporting a congregation where God is the central focus and where worship invites surrender to this God. I cannot support worship as a means to serve people and meet their perceived needs and wants. This practice marginalizes God or makes God altogether unnecessary.

Paul, please excuse my audacity; I do not wish to be offensive, but I must be clear. I believe the new mission being proposed, built on church-growth principles, will lead to a gathering of people who inadvertently dismiss God from their life as a congregation. By attending to their own perceived needs and the insatiable appetite to be fulfilled by getting more, they forsake the only source of hope that can touch their true need—the need to be loved. I do not think we need a new mission to fulfill this objective. The consumerist society in which we live has mastered this mission quite well. As congregations assume this church-growth orientation, they will not likely be able, even with the best intentions and a huge investment of money and energy, to out-market the professional marketers.

I am aware of some of the responses to this point of view. You might ask, "Don't we need to meet people where they are and then bring them along, teach them to surrender themselves?" This is the strategy used by those who advocate "seeker services": find the way by which you can at least attract people, and begin there. The theory assumes that once a person encounters an inspiring and affirming community that promises, implicitly if not explicitly, to meet their needs and make them happy, they will grow in their faith and mature to ever deeper levels of faithfulness, which will eventually include surrender to Jesus.

Two aspects of this theory trouble me. First, the way a person initially bonds to a community will normally be the way they remain connected. The way missionaries entered their foreign mission fields provides an example: for many years, missionaries were sent overseas and initially spent time with other missionaries in a language school. For the rest of their stay, they longed to leave their local assignments and return to those with whom they had first bonded. So someone tried an experiment. When missionaries arrived, they immediately were sent to their mission post and began their work. Months later, they gathered with other missionaries for language school. These missionaries could not wait to return to those they first joined.

We must be careful about the way people bond to congregations. Do they bond to the unstated but too often present promise that their needs will be met? Or do they join expecting to wrestle with a God who challenges them to surrender and lose themselves? Changing from one perspective to another will be difficult, if not impossible.

Also, changing direction midstream could seem manipulative, shattering trust and producing alienation and anger. Often, in our culture of sophisticated consumers, any hint of bait-and-switch will drive people away. People want honesty. They deserve to know what they are getting involved in. Seeking people out, promising to fill their needs, and then, once they have invested themselves, challenging them to leave behind their needs and focus on God, will foster a community of faith full of distrust and conflict.

Again, I don't intend this to be taken personally, but I cannot support a mission start based on this ineffective and dishonest practice.

Another attempt to respond to concerns I have raised has been the now common practice of "alternative worship." Normally practiced in established congregations, this involves having more than one style of worship available. The most strident example of this practice involves providing a "seeker service" (as well as a more traditional service) on each Sunday morning, with a style relevant to a particular market niche. Even when the polar opposites of traditional worship and seeker worship are not practiced, it has become common for two different styles of worship services to be offered each Sunday. Multiple worship styles have become a sign of a congregation's health and its willingness to spread the gospel. Even new congregations are being formed with more than one style of worship on Sunday. This way they can reach more than one segment of the market.

At least two concerns cause me to draw the line and refuse to endorse this practice. First, the way we worship profoundly shapes the God we come to know. Our knowledge and experience of God is always limited, but worship is the primary way that limited knowledge is revealed. Alternative worship makes it possible for me to decide which God I want to experience. One week I may want a contemporary God, another time, a traditional God. When I can choose God, God is no longer God. Worship demands I encounter a God who makes a claim on me. Worship challenges my deeply held conviction that I can be in charge of my life. When I cannot choose how to worship, but must let the worship make its claim on me, I may not like what I experience. I may be challenged and provoked. I may be surprised and filled with awe and wonder. Worship confronts me with a God over whom I have no control and cannot choose. Providing alternative worship experiences on a Sunday morning makes it nearly impossible to know the radical joy of losing oneself to the God who has chosen us.

Second, the ritual life of a community provides the way for character to be formed. A congregation with a variety of worship styles available on a Sunday morning will find it nearly impossible to shape communal character. More often than not, conflict and competition will arise in these congregations. If worship becomes nothing more than a matter of my personal preference, then, because worship is the core of a congregation's being, all aspects of congregational life become extensions of every member's personal desire. Only the hard work of leaders, who spend their time trying to hold it all together by their own personal charm or by providing an ever-expanding menu of options, can deter the conflict. When leaders find this to be the focus of their time and energy, they have again been distracted from attending to what is most important to God and God's will for God's people. I wonder if this is not one of the primary reasons for the burnout of leaders, both lay and clergy.

Notice that in all I have said, I do not advocate one particular style of worship. In and of themselves, the questions of whether to use contemporary liturgies, praise music, or polka masses are not why I draw the line. I am troubled by the assumptions that undergird these and other choices. I am concerned that all missions begin with surrender to God and not focusing on oneself. Paying careful attention to this concern is of more importance than the questions we ask as we plan worship. I am convinced that as we wrestle with these issues, we will discover the appropriate styles of worship given a specific context.

Thank you for asking me this great question, "Is your conviction about church growth enough of a reason to not support the spreading of the gospel of Jesus Christ?"

To this question, I must respond, Yes. Here I must draw the line. For me, my role as a pastor involves unfolding the character of a congregation, which invites people to surrender to Jesus and to relinquish even their deepest needs to the reign of God he has made flesh. A congregation founded on church-growth principles seems contrary to that vision. So here I must take a stand.

If and when we, as churches in this community, discern that God is calling us to begin a mission that will move beyond church-growth principles, I will be eager to be part of that conversation. I, like you, desire for the gospel of Jesus Christ to be spread to all. I just don't believe the new mission, in its present formulation, will fulfill this deep desire.

7

TO BE A CHANGE AGENT:
BE A TRADITIONAL PASTOR WITH A TWIST

The winter theological conference was an annual event that Pastor Stephens loyally attended every year. In many ways, he looked forward to the gathering. The conversation and a chance to catch up on what was happening with colleagues was almost worth the time. And if by chance the conference included something challenging, provocative, or even useful, he considered it a bonus.

Over the years, the bonuses seemed to be fewer and harder to come by. Not to say that the event wasn't well-planned and publicized. The advertising brochures became flashier while the event itself grew duller and more disconnected from his understanding and practice of ministry. There seemed to be little attention to the Bible or theology. These gatherings touted "practical" stuff. And practical apparently meant working very hard to discourage pastors by telling them they weren't doing a good job and that they had to do ministry differently. If they did not change, they were not only being unfaithful to God and the church, but their denomination would continue to lose members. Someone even called it "losing market share" once, a moment of unintentional honesty.

This year's brochure proclaimed, in bright colors on glossy paper: "Be a Change Agent—Before It's Too Late." Probably written by some well-paid Director of Discouragement, thought Pastor Stephens.

Pastor Stephens attended the conference warily and discovered that the contact with old friends was indeed worth the price of admission. But beyond that, things kind of unraveled. He longed for good worship, but too often the worship reflected the setting: a hotel conference room. The worship reminded him of the broccoli served at hotel banquets: limp, overcooked, and mostly added for color instead of taste or nutrition.

Pastor Stephens went to a few sessions. The speakers all seemed to say the same thing: The world is changing and the church must change. You as leaders must force your congregation to change. If it doesn't change, it will die. Churches that don't change will move from being mainline churches to sideline churches (which has already happened), and inevitably, finally, to dead churches (which is just around the corner). And you, pastor, are responsible for stopping this domino effect.

Two common phrases dominated the presentations. First, all congregations seemed to suffer from the "we have always done it that way" disease. One presentation, based on this well-worked mantra, was entitled "The Seven Last Words of the Church." The presenter spent an hour expounding the cliché. He consistently spoke of congregations as the enemy and the problem. If congregations would just shape up, then ministry could happen and the church would no longer be a humiliated sideline (or worse, dead) church. The implied message, sometimes stated explicitly, was that it was the pastor's task to shape up the church.

The other phrase that came up again and again, although usually much more subtly stated, went something like this: "Theology doesn't matter; it is practice that is important." One lecture had a subsection titled: "They do not care how much you know, they want to know how much you care." The presenter quickly betrayed his anti-intellectual bias. During the questions time, when asked about the theological implications of his practice, he dismissed the question as irrelevant and wondered if theology wasn't a place where pastors who were afraid of change liked to hide.

Even in past years when the conference presenters struck a chord with Pastor Stephens, he would plan to miss a session and spend some quiet time in his room. This was his opportunity to read some periodicals he had not been able to look at and to simply be still. At this conference, it was not hard for him to break away. He could not stand much more unintentional shaming, and he longed to return to the vocation of parish pastor. He chuckled to himself as he drifted away to his room. "I suppose I am hiding away from being a change agent," he thought.

Pastor Stephens found himself caught up in an article about a Lutheran congregation in the Bible Belt that was seeking to claim its Lutheran identity. Their ministry was vital and even growing. Being a traditional Lutheran parish seemed to be the key to their mission. They worked at making their worship more formal, not less. The pastor emphasized the Word and Sacrament in his ministry. Working against the wisdom of the prophets of change, the congregation reached out and touched people by being radical—that is, true to their roots. Perhaps, thought Pastor Stephens, this Bible Belt experience was transferable to almost all North American settings.

Could it be that Lutherans and mainline Christians as a whole, seeking to claim an identity in an alien land, might find that identity in being radical, that is, deeply rooted in their tradition? He got so involved in the implications of the thought that he arrived late for lunch.

Some friends had saved him a place at the table. The lively table conversation focused on what the others had just heard in the session Pastor Stephens had missed. The speaker challenged the pastors to be change agents. Working from sociological and psychological concepts (rather than biblical insights), pastors were told that as the key leaders in congregations, they had to make change happen. Pastors needed to push and challenge their congregation, because the congregation will always seek the status quo. Real leaders, according to this approach, pull congregations into the future. They dare to challenge and provoke congregations. Leaders make ministry happen in spite of the congregation.

Pastor Stephens listened to the comments and was glad he had taken a break. He could not stand much more advice and counsel about how he had to become different. He thought to himself, "Perhaps I am the one who is reluctant and resistant. Maybe I am alone in the feeling that all this change is happening in spite of me."

But then Sara broke into the conversation. She didn't speak up often, but when she did, even the most vociferous in the crowd would stop and listen.

"What was interesting to me," she said, "was the contradiction of the first premise of the presenter with his ending challenge to us. He began by asserting a foundational principle. He began by stating that the higher the level of anxiety in an organism or organization, the lower the level of adaptability. In other words, the more anxious we are, the less we are able to change and adapt. When the congregations we serve are highly anxious and afraid, they are not able to change. Instead, they turn inward, stay stuck, and lose their courage to claim the future. Speaking biblically—something the presenter did not do—I wonder if this is why so often the first thing God speaks, through angels and prophets and Jesus, when God breaks into the world in transforming ways, is 'Do not be afraid.' Is this why Jesus taught the disciples not to be anxious?"

She paused and then continued: "The contradiction occurred when the presenter shared that concept, then focused on how we as pastors, as leaders, should challenge, push, and demand that our congregations change. In fact, if I understand how this works, such forcing of change only raises the level of anxiety, thus lowering the possibility of fostering the very change that is sought. Does that make sense?"

For a while only the scraping of silverware on plates was heard. Then someone said, "Wow! That makes great sense. But what does it mean for us?"

Before anyone could respond, an announcement was made that the conference would reconvene in ten minutes. A conversation with the bishop was next on the schedule.

Pastor Stephens heard the bishop speak, but he was not really listening. He was thinking about the luncheon conversation. He wasn't sure what was discussed with the bishop, but he felt the anxiety in the room rise, and continue to rise as the conversation between the bishop and the pastors seemed to get more desperate. "If Sara's theory was right," he thought, "not much change will take place here today." Pastor Stephens prayed that an angel might come, enter the room, and announce the age-old message, "Be not afraid."

Somewhat immodestly, Pastor Stephens asked himself, "If I were bishop, how would I lower anxiety, rather than raise it? How would I relieve this community of fear so that change, real change, could happen?" But then, on the table in front of him, he wrote something that applied more readily to him: "How can I as a pastor lower anxiety rather than raise it? How can I relieve the congregation I serve of fear so that change, real change, can happen?"

The bishop closed his presentation by asking the question he always asked, "Is there anything I or my staff can do to assist you in your ministry?" Pastor Stephens almost asked the question that had been nagging at him for years. Now, however, he had found a new way of asking the question. "Could you find ways to proclaim the gospel to me, again and again and again? I get anxious, afraid, discouraged, and feel alone. I need to hear the gospel. I need a pastor who proclaims the Word of God to me. Without this, I am too afraid and anxious to be changed." But he held the question. "Perhaps I'm the only one who feels this way," he thought.

Pastor Stephens did not hear much of the last presentation—something titled: "Demanding Pastors Make Successful Churches." Instead, he was attempting to answer his own questions. He was musing about what his ministry would look like if he focused on lowering anxiety, not demanding (to use a word echoing throughout the room) change. The simplicity of this notion awed him and fired his imagination and excitement for ministry.

The presenter kept repeating the phrase, "Demand to expand," like a football coach rallying the team to go and win the big one. Pastor Stephens did not get caught up in the frenzy but instead wrote a summary statement at the bottom of his notes, "To be a change agent, be a traditional pastor with a twist." He considered the practice of being a traditional pastor. Preaching, presiding, praying, pastoral care: in other words, through word and deed, proclaiming the gospel.

At home the next morning at breakfast, Pastor Stephens's wife finally dared to ask about the conference. It usually took a day or two for him to recover. He would more often than not come home discouraged, angry, depressed, and demoralized. But this time she noticed something different. There was a sparkle in his eyes, a lift in his step, and a sense of joy that overflowed.

She had rarely seen this in recent years. Yet she could remember his time in seminary and early in his ordained ministry. Then he had used to rave that there was nothing more satisfying and joyous than being a pastor. She hadn't heard those words for years.

He told her about the friends he had seen. He told some jokes he had heard. A bit of gossip was shared about which pastors were interviewing and with what congregations. Finally, she ventured into the awkward discussion. "How were the presentations? Did you learn anything?"

Pastor Stephens smiled. "They were flashy, well-prepared, even entertaining. But mostly they were demoralizing, as usual. But the irony is, their attempt to beat me down did not win the day this time. I left the conference renewed, committed, and excited to be a pastor. At the conference, I was convicted of what I had forgotten: that I am called to be a pastor. I am called to preach the gospel of Jesus that offers unconditional hope. I am called to administer, not the congregation, but the sacraments, which are a visible word of grace. I am called to teach, not organizational and psychological processes, but Bible stories of a God who continually transforms all the world, because this God will not quit on us until all of creation is redeemed."

Pastor Stephens's wife looked confused. It sounded so simple. Isn't this what he had been doing for years? Why did he find renewal in these insights? It seemed so plain, so ordinary, so basic.

Then he looked at her, his face radiant and his body poised for action. He looked at her and could read her mind. He quieted a bit and spoke confessionally: "Over the years, I have forgotten to trust God to work through these simple acts. Simple pastoral acts of preaching, presiding, teaching, and praying are the means God uses to redeem the world. I have kept doing these things, but I have forgotten to be expectant. I have forgotten that when the gospel is proclaimed and there is an encounter with Jesus, change, real transformative change, will take place. I have been so concerned with pushing for change that I have forgotten to preach, teach, preside, and get out of the way. Or, more often than not, I have felt so guilty about not pushing for change, as I have been continually encouraged to do, that I have lost my passion.

"The conference speakers hit on the old truth: the higher the level of anxiety, the lower the level of adaptability. I know that to be true. And what is more, I am convinced that nothing lowers anxiety in a congregation like the presence of a traditional pastor who preaches the gospel, administers the sacraments, and teaches the Bible. I came away from the conference thrilled and honored to be a traditional pastor, but now with a new twist. The twist is my renewed expectancy. The twist is that I seek to trust and live this truth: proclaiming the gospel, and trusting its power, is the means for transformation and change to happen."

Then Pastor Stephens stood tall before his wife in his favorite mocking, exaggerated-preacher pose, and he cried out in a deep sermonic tenor, as if to proclaim some miraculous event, "Take a look at me. An everyday traditional pastor with a twist. What you see is a *real* radical change agent."

8

CONGREGATIONAL CONFLICT: SACRED VIOLENCE

Like a wound festering and infected, the pain started as an irritation but became unbearable. When the pain demanded attention, three people made phone calls. First the congregational president called the bishop and pleaded for help. Soon, the pastor called and made a similar plea. Was it possible for someone to assist in sorting out what was happening? Finally, the bishop called me. As assistant to the bishop, could I go and intervene? As judicatory officials, it was our task to try to help.

At the bishop's office, we expected some relationships between pastors and congregations would end in pain and sorrow. Some were doomed to fail from the beginning. However, we assumed that this pastor and congregation relationship was a success. The pastor had served in this parish for a number of years. From all accounts, his ministry had been effective until very recently. For us, that meant we received few, if any, complaints from either the pastor or his congregation. Each year when the pastor was asked if he was interested in moving, he indicated that he continued to feel called to lead this congregation, and there was still ministry left for him to do. Each year the congregation agreed, and even rewarded him with an increase in salary.

The rumblings, quiet at first, had started a few months earlier. Little things became irritants. The pastor dealt with these difficulties as he always had. Through the power of his person and hard work, he showed how much he cared and how committed he was to the people. As the irritations began to grow into difficulties and then into all-out conflict, the pastor worked harder and harder, cared more and more, and let the congregation know how painful all this was to him, and how he loved them so much.

Finally, the conflict came to a head around the Sunday school Christmas program. The new Sunday school superintendent wanted to make a change. Instead of just retelling the story, she wanted to tell the story through a little drama she had found. The Sunday school superintendent was a new member, which meant that she had joined within the last four years. When she and her family joined, it was a real coup. They were the kind of new members every pastor and congregation longs to receive. In order to make sure they joined, the pastor and his family made a special effort to become good friends with them, and they often socialized together.

The congregation did not respond well to the new Christmas program idea. Teachers and members of the Education Board told the pastor of their dismay. Whenever the pastor heard a complaint, he followed his tried-and-true strategy. He immediately sought out the person or persons who were upset and worked to make them feel good. If all else failed, he would turn the conversation to his many years of being their pastor and their common friendship. Certainly he would do everything a friend could do to make things okay. The message was clear: he hadn't failed up to now and they could count on him. He would make everything okay.

This strategy had served the pastor well, but it surely was hard. To hold the congregation together by the power of his affection and commitment meant working many, many hours. The strategy was dependent on his obsessive attention and would fail if there was any doubt about his commitment and care. More than once, he cut short a vacation or broke a family commitment to attend to some congregational concern.

Now it seemed that this pastoral strategy was failing. Like a Minnesota lake, which freezes overnight, the climate of the congregation had changed rapidly from tranquillity to a chilling discomfort. No matter how he tried, the pastor could not address the problem. It was as if there were not enough hours in the day to be present with all who were upset. It felt as if his arms were stretched to the extreme, yet he could not provide his compassionate touch to everyone who had come to expect it. His inability to make it all work only fueled the conflict. People had expected his unfailing presence and friendship. Now he seemed to have forgotten them, and it seemed he just didn't care anymore. Their disappointment turned to hurt, then to anger. I learned quickly that the conflict was not about a Christmas program. It was about a troubled relationship, mired in disappointment.

This cycle of disappointment-hurt-anger was also present in the pastor. Actually, the pastor did not exhibit any of these traits. The only way he knew how to respond was to work harder, care more, and show his commitment through greater sacrifice. To exhibit disappointment, hurt, or anger would undo all the hard work he had done. It was his spouse who lived the cycle. Her disappointment in the congregation was clear to anyone who had any contact with her. She was hurt as she watched her husband frantically giving himself away again and again. She was angry that the congregation would turn on them after all they had sacrificed. How could they betray his love?

This is what I learned as I listened to as many people as possible during my visit, my intervention. I experienced a congregation unable to understand why they were experiencing deep disappointment, a congregation hurt and angry, focused on a pastor they loved and called a friend. I experienced a pastor, and a pastor's family, who had the same feelings about a congregation, a group of people, who they loved and claimed as friends. Many times people shook their heads and said, "I can't figure out what happened. It just doesn't make sense. Why can't it be like it used to be?"

Returning to a motel room after a late-night conversation with the pastor and his wife, I picked up the book I had been reading, *Sacred Violence: Paul's Hermeneutic of the Cross*, by Robert G.

Hamerton-Kelly,[1] which uses the hermeneutic of René Girard to explore Paul's theology of the cross. I was reading, as I often do, with no specific application of the material in mind. Continuing to deepen my understanding of a theology of the cross is a passion for me. The book looked interesting and did not disappoint me. As I settled in for the night, I looked forward to leaving behind the crisis that had demanded my attention all day. A little theoretical consideration of the cross sounded, in its own odd way, refreshing.

Only a page into my reading, I was drawn back into the congregational conflict I had just left. Hamerton-Kelly was explaining René Girard's theory of mimetic desire. As I read and absorbed what was being described, I realized I had been experiencing this theory in the present conflict.

Hamerton-Kelly writes about Girard:

> The configuration of desire is triangular, therefore, running from the subject through the mediator to the object. The angles at the base of the triangle can be large or small; the larger they are the farther the distance between the plane of the subject and the plane of the mediator, and vice-versa. When the distance is relatively far the imitation is relatively untrammeled by rivalry; Girard calls this the state of "external mediation." When the distance is relatively near the imitation becomes rivalrous; Girard call this "internal meditation." As the plane of the mediator approaches the plane of the subject, rivalry grows with an intensity inversely proportionate to the diminishing distance. Eventually the mediator becomes an obstacle and the subject shifts attention from the object to the mediator/obstacle. Thus mimesis becomes mimetic rivalry. What was an imitative aspiration for the object becomes a direct rivalry between the imitators.[2]

I read these words and felt like Hameton-Kelly had been by my side observing the past day of congregational conflict. I read on:

> When the mediator arrives on the same plane as the subject, he or she stands between the subject and object, and thus the instigator of desire is the obstacle to its fulfillment. At this point the subject wishes to destroy the obstacle, but cannot do so without destroying the instigator of desire and thus its own reason for being. The

> desire of the mediator created the value in the first place and thus
> called forth the subject's desire; therefore in order to maintain
> itself desire must maintain the mediator as obstacle. Desire needs
> a rival to survive, because its fulfillment is its end.[3]

I read on for just a few paragraphs, and a sentence stuck out
that shaped how I would understand the present conflict and how
I might intervene in a helpful way. "Human being is constituted
relationally—that is, transcendentally—and the state of mimetic
rivalry is the pathology of a 'deviated transcendence,' of a desire
that should be aroused from a truly transcendent spiritual source
but instead is aroused by the immanent neighbor."[4]

I put down my book and began to imagine how to proceed.

The next day I encouraged and challenged the pastor to resign
his present call. Because he was so fused with the congregation, it
would be impossible for him to again function as their pastor. His
love and commitment to the congregation meant that, despite the
pain and hurt, this counsel was difficult and extremely painful.
And although the congregation was unhappy with the pastor,
once my recommendation to the pastor was made public, the congregation turned their anger and frustration on me. Recalling the
insights of Girard explained by Hamerton-Kelly, this scapegoating
was understandable and unavoidable. I attempted not to try to fix
or quiet the anger but to accept it as necessary.

My commitment to the pastor and his family included teaching them about the dynamics that led to the present conflict. If
the pastor pursued the same style of ministry in the next pastoral
setting, in all likelihood, the same painful and violent end would
come of his ministry. He and his family must understand that
fusing with the congregation leads to conflict. In order to function as the mediator of the sacred, it is essential to maintain a
critical distance while also remaining connected. The coaching of
the pastor around these issues involved deepening a commitment
to do ministry out of his office and not his person. It meant nur-
turing a deeper trust in the transformative powers of the primary

symbols of the church: sacraments, preaching, liturgy. Doing ministry through these symbols provides a means of mediating effectively and maintaining distance. The coaching included a challenge to find supportive friendships outside the congregation and to resist the temptation to become an "immanent neighbor" to those who are being served. Finally, the coaching involved standing with the pastor and his family so that they might accept, painful as it would be, that loneliness and being marginalized is a necessary reality for the faithful practice of ministry. I continually reminded them of the deep hurt they experienced when they lost their liminality. Compared to this pain, and the way the conflict inhibited the witness of the gospel, present experiences of loneliness and being an outsider were minimal.

Addressing the congregation was at least as complicated. The hurt, disappointment, and rage were real and evident to everyone. What made it so difficult was that there was no effective way to rationally explain what had happened. I encouraged and, as much as I could, insisted that a new permanent pastor be called as soon as possible. If it were possible, I would have had the bishop appoint a pastor almost immediately. The congregation did not presently have the health to make good decisions, yet the only way toward this health was with a permanent pastor in place. The new pastor would then have been coached and encouraged to understand his or her role as a mediator. Keeping critical distance and mediating the transcendent power of the sacred would be key to the congregation's healing. The congregation did not need to go through a complicated healing process, or understand what had happened, or take time to grieve. They needed to begin to trust a pastor who would function as a mediator of the sacred. They had lost contact not just with the former pastor, but with God. Until that contact is reestablished, conflict will continue to fester. Only a mediator they can learn to trust and depend upon can make this happen.

Now, many years later as a parish pastor, I often recall my experience in that congregation and the insights I gained from my reading that night in the motel. Every time I find myself narrowing the angle and losing my distance from the congregation I serve, I remember the pain and suffering that happens when a pastor becomes an "immanent neighbor" with the congregation. I recall the words one of the congregational members spoke to me during the intervention. "We called a pastor and then made him into a good friend. When it was too late, we found out what we really needed was not another friend, but a pastor." The congregation I serve does not need me to be their friend. They need me to be their pastor. If I forget this truth, I will likely end up in the midst of congregational conflict: sacred violence.

9

EACH CONGREGATION: ONE PASTOR

A cryptic comment began the musing that has come to be a firm conviction. The bishop returned from a meeting of a taskforce called "The Study of Ministry." They had spent time exploring the many ways ministry was ordered internationally. They had discovered that the fastest-growing and most vital churches in the world have a shortage of clergy. Reflecting on this fact, the bishop made the off-hand comment that challenged me to consider a new concept. He said, "Maybe our problem is that we have too many pastors."

Now, nearly ten years later, I am convinced of a truth embedded within that comment. I am so convinced that I try to practice the truth. I serve a basically blue-collar congregation of nearly 1,700 members in a small Midwestern city. I have chosen to be the only ordained member of the staff. The congregation continues to grow in depth of character and boldness of witness as well as in the number of those God has sent to be part of the community. There are likely many reasons for the blessings God has bestowed upon the congregation. Yet I am convinced a major reason for the present relative health of the congregation is a public and intentional choice to be a congregation with only one ordained pastor.

The thesis that provides the foundation for this conviction and practice is as follows:

For congregational witness to be boldly evangelical (that is, bearing witness to the kingdom of God for the sake of the world), congregations must have a strong, compassionate, courageous, and clearly identified leader. When this essential leadership role is divided and shared, the evangelical mission of the church suffers greatly. When there is conflict, thus division among ordained staff, this is obvious. I am proposing that even when the relationship between multiple ordained members of a staff is healthy and strong, it inhibits the very leadership the ordained are called to provide.

I know this is a challenging thesis for a church built on the assumptions of modernity. One pastoral leader smacks of hierarchy and seems to diminish the role of others in the ministry. I would contend that the opposite is true. My experience, both through observation of others and through trial and error on my own, has confirmed the fact that strong leaders attract other strong leaders. The opposite is also true. Weak leaders who abdicate their roles, or confusion about who is the leader, drive away those who wish to use their leadership gifts.

Let me take a moment to explain what I see as the forces that drive congregations to seek out more than one ordained pastor and the rationale for proposing each congregation be served by one ordained pastor.

1. The proliferation of pastoral staff developed as a natural result of the modern fascination with the pastor as manager. The pastor's primary focus is on meeting people's needs and providing programs. For this reason, the more pastors who could be made available, the more contact there will be with the congregational members, who are the primary consumers or clients. More pastors on staff also means a more thorough and elaborate bureaucracy. More pastors allows for more complicated flowcharts, job descriptions, policies, and meetings. For the modern organization, these functions are trophies that indicate success and growth.

If, however, the primary focus of the pastor is toward God for the sake of continually refocusing the community so that it might be a witness, then one clearly identified leader will be more effective. No matter how united and singular of heart and mind a pastoral staff is (and achieving such a state takes tremendous time, energy, and resources), the staff will inevitably point in different directions. This lack of clear focus, no matter how subtle, will be a distraction to the clarity of vision needed to challenge congregations to the bold and daring gospel witness.

2. The Constantinian vision of the church as a cherished part of the empire demanded pastors who would be more chaplains than prophets. Prophetic ministry challenged the dominant culture,[1] whereas chaplaincy ministry nurtures and supports the organic development of faith that happened simply by existing in the western world in a Christian country. Again, the proliferation of pastors in a church supported the illusion of an ever-expanding Christian society. The logical result is the notion that the more pastors (who are the "expert" Christians) in a congregation, the more faithful and religious it has become. Like expanding retail outlets indicate the growth of business, because more people are aligning themselves with its products, so more pastors indicate the same for a church.

However, for those of us whose Constantinian worldview has been shattered, buttressing up and trying to recover an empire church is an empty and passionless mission. The wondrous challenge for a post-Constantinian church is to be faithful as a remnant people. Unfolding the character of congregations willing to embrace this mission demands a leader who will inspire trust, courage, and conviction on the part of the followers. For a congregation to become a movement more than an institution, it needs a leader who calls it forth in mission.

In spite of the troubling images associated with it, a military example may be helpful. The Constantinian church is like an army reserve unit involved in summer exercises. They go away to practice what it would be like to be in a battle if and when it ever happens. The absence of a real enemy means they can share leadership. They might even have meetings to decide who will be in charge on what day or for what tasks. The followers are not anxious about the continual change of who is in charge. They feel no threat and are in danger of losing little. They may prefer one leader to another. But as long as a minimal level of competence and authority is in place, the followers adjust just fine.

When, however, an army unit faces a real enemy and must engage in battle, there is no time for meetings and discussion and deciding who is in charge. Someone must take command. There is great danger if a lack of decisiveness and a foggy sense of vision is present. At these times, one strong, trusted, capable, authorized leader is needed. The followers will be empowered to do what they are called to do when such a leader is in place and the mission is clear. The post-Constantinian church now faces a real spiritual battle. We are no longer preparing for an imaginary enemy. Congregations are set aside by God to engage this world with a message of profound hope, shared with deep love and compassion. This is demanding work, and for this mission to be effective, a congregation needs a leader whom it can trust and whom it is willing to follow. In the absence of such a leader, or in the diffusion of that leadership to many people, the congregation will become anxious, afraid, and timid, and will often refuse to carry out the mission. The likely result of this fear will include, among other things, turning on the leader with accusations of ineffectiveness and incompetence.

3. Congregations desire more than one pastor. Unconsciously, having more than one pastor supports the natural quest for homeostasis (the status quo). When there is more than one pastor, if one pastor's challenge to the congregation seems too difficult, there is always another pastor to turn to. "Good pastor–bad pastor" (a variation of "good cop–bad cop") is often played. Usually this "game" begins to attract enough communal emotive energy that the conflict becomes personal, and the pastor who draws the straw of playing "bad pastor" on a particular issue begins to fester with resentment. As conflict begins to grow, the congregation, again unconsciously, is relieved. For as painful as

they find the internal conflict, focusing on the internal conflict will call them to little substantial change, and the status quo will remain. Deep down, change is what they fear. Deep down, change is why they need a leader who cannot be so easily, however unconsciously, manipulated.

When a pastoral staff works well—when they get along well and experience strong bonds of collegiality—it takes tremendous effort and energy. Again unconsciously, the congregation finds this easy to support. For when the institutional time and energy is consumed by team-building and maintaining relationships among the leaders, the resources available to challenge the congregation are minimized. Certainly, all staff teams will need to attend to their internal dynamics. But maintaining relationships among ordained staff demands an extensive amount of time and energy because of the unique leadership role they play.

Having only one pastor per congregation mitigates this quest for homeostasis. The congregation and other staff are forced to deal with their leader. They cannot run to another leader when they do not get what they want. Having one pastor per congregation focuses their reluctance and allows this resistive energy to be used to promote continual conversion and daring witness. In fact, it is precisely this conflict that James McGregor Burns[2] and Robert Fritz[3] claim as the essential ingredient for leadership. Without the conflict, there would be no reason to change. Having one pastor per congregation focuses the conflict and facilitates the potential for the transformation essential for gospel witness.

4. Pastors like to serve with other pastors. This is the flip side to the above reality. Having more than one pastor supports the leader in the unconscious, natural quest for homeostasis (the status quo). When difficult issues or people arise for one pastor on a pastoral team, he or she can always hand them off to another pastor. In fact, pastoral staffs are often built with this in mind. One pastor is not good at relating to a certain kind of people, so another, complementary pastor is found. The unintended result

is that all pastors involved are relieved of the opportunity to struggle and learn from the stranger, the outsider, the "enemy." This encourages the understanding of pastors as providing certain commodities (or being a commodity) to meet the needs of the congregation. This is a death blow to evangelical witness.

When there is but one pastor, there is no choice. The pastor must relate to all the congregation. The pastor cannot run away from the difficult, awkward, and challenging people and the opportunities for ministry these people provide. Parallel process—the principle that what happens in and with the leader is mirrored in the congregation—would indicate that the extent to which the pastor cannot run away from his or her struggles will be reflected in the congregation's openness to engaging in the difficult, the awkward, and the challenging opportunities for witness. To modify the old adage, "Conflict is an occasion for conversation," the church might say, "Conflict is an occasion for bold witness." Having one pastor provides the possibility that conflict and struggle can be redemptive, in a way that having multiple pastors on a staff cannot.

The proposal that each congregation be served by one pastor can overcome the pressure of the status quo if we dare to focus on the mission to which congregations are called. Congregations are a "God-gathered people who bear witness to the gospel in all that they say and do, for the sake of the world."[4] Following are some reasons this mission is emboldened when a congregation is served by one pastor.

1. A congregation challenged boldly to mission and witness must have confidence in its leader. Without confidence and trust in a leader, the congregation will experience a failure of nerve when it needs it most. If the mission of the congregation is to meet the needs of people (which usually means "people like me with needs like mine"), there is no need for confidence. Instead, a good marketing plan and good sales associates (pastors) will do the job: "Hello, my name is Pastor Jim, and I am here to serve

you." The more people on the streets, the better the chance to make a sale and fill a need.

However, if the congregation is called to witness the kingdom of God as an anticipatory community,[5] claiming an evangelical vision through daring communal action that is countercultural and in tension with the world at large, then there must be confidence in the leader. This mission is frightening and demands continually being connected with the leader to rebuild the conviction that we are truly being what God calls us to be. Often in this situation, the congregation will wish it had some other pastor toward whom to turn. Often, the pastor will feel overwhelmed by the responsibility to lead people into the struggle. But there is no way out. They must be together.

Thus the congregation must hear regularly, for the most part, weekly, from its pastor. Not only the common message is important, but also the common presence. Congregations empowered for bold witness have confidence in their leaders and gain that confidence through the proclamation of the Word. To say it simply, in order to instill courage for mission and witness, congregations need one preacher.

2. A parade of pastors through the chancel, dissecting liturgy as if parceling out time at a time-share condo, leaves the congregation with a cacophony of voices rather than a singular clarion call toward God. And, if that ritual actualizes our deepest values, dividing the liturgical functions of community often results in the compartmentalization of the congregation. Separating preaching and presiding is the most common and troublesome practice when there is more than one ordained leader in a congregation. An effective pastoral leader needs to continually wrestle with how to both support and challenge a congregation. A pastor must have at his or her disposal all the resources to provoke the congregation to be moved forward. Dividing the presiding and the preaching reduces both the singular focus and the unified mobilization of resources. It may be entertaining to have different voices, but though enter-

tained, the congregation will not likely be provoked toward emboldened witness.

A congregation needs one presider who also preaches. This presider must call the community together (invocation), proclaim a faithful vision (preach), continually remind the community whose name they bear (do the washing of baptisms), provide nourishment and sustenance for the journey (serve at the table), and offer the blessing (benediction). A singular voice, a singular presence, brings unity to the liturgy and to the community. A singular voice more likely minimizes confusion and focuses the congregation for action.

3. A congregation with one pastor will soon have to decide what is necessary for that pastor to do and what can be done by others. This defining process liberates all involved. In fact, the pastor is likely to find himself or herself with more time to be a leader and less need to be a manager. With more ordained pastors serving a congregation, the congregation will perceive that ministry is done by those set apart. People normally assume that those who are paid need to do their jobs, and resentment surfaces when those "hired" try to get others involved. Reversing this perception is difficult if not impossible.

When there is only one pastor, the congregation more easily understands the demands on his or her time. Soon they must wrestle individually and as a community about priorities. The pastor can easily shape this conversation and graciously identify what is central and essential. If nothing else, fostering this conversation is worth embracing the experiment of one pastor for each congregation. The process can be one of those old "values clarification" exercises. Given the reality of limited time and energy, what are the most valued things a pastor needs to do to serve God faithfully through this congregation? More important than the congregation's response, the pastor will have to decide what to let go of and what to hold on to. This intentional and public move toward definition will make the pastoral leader more effective; the congregation, like all organisms, finds those who are clearly defined more attractive than those who are not.

4. One pastor for each congregation provides a climate in which the virtues of the ordained can be deepened. William Willimon, commenting on pastoral character, writes, "True morality—the ability to judge our own self-perception, the gift of seeing things in perspective—comes from the practices outside those sanctioned by the system. It comes from being forced, Sunday after Sunday, to lead and to pray the Prayer of Confession followed by the Words of Absolution. It comes from being ordered, Sunday after Sunday, to 'Do this in remembrance of me.' In my case it comes from being forced, Sunday after Sunday, to march in to church behind a cross, rather than behind a flag, my list of publications, or my pension portfolio."[6] If you are the only pastor, you cannot escape these practices. I would add one more to Willimon's list: Week after week, if you are the only pastor, you will have to wrestle with the text and allow that text to become incarnate within you. For there is no one else to preach! When one preaches, the urgent imposition of the text upon one's life is strong and demanding. This shapes pastoral virtue. To say it another way, when a pastor preaches occasionally (not nearly every Sunday), it is dangerous and can easily lead to the decay of pastoral character.

One pastor for each congregation might provide the best and most effective way to renew passion and commitment for evangelical leadership. The things the church must do, those things that make the church distinctively the church, will, out of necessity, receive the greatest attention by its leader. Proclamation, worship, and witness are foundational to the church. If only one pastor serves the congregation, he or she must attend to these central tasks. Such attention will continually develop the character of the leader and the congregation.

5. When it happens—and it does happen on occasion—that pastors on a team develop strong relationships with each other,

they are tempted to refrain from involvement in the wider church, in collegial relationships outside the pastoral team. This type of enmeshment often results in the kind of destructive parochialism that turns congregations inward and domesticates the gospel witness.

One pastor per congregation has the potential to increase the loneliness and thus deepen the vulnerability and need for pastors to move outside of their competitive posture and become partners in the wider mission of the church. From another perspective, if and when the church focuses on recovering the ministerium, the practice of one pastor per parish will be more viable.

6. Finally, one must address the concern of hierarchy and power. Is this not just a ploy to put pastors back on the pedestal and consolidate authority? Is this proposal not rooted in a deep longing to recover the status and position that has been lost? What does this proposal say about the ministry of the laity? Does not more focus on the pastor discourage lay involvement? And what about collegiality and teamwork among the staff?

The style a pastor chooses to claim is the most significant determinant in the use of the pastoral office for the grasping of power and authority. Those who have a need to climb on the pedestal and take control will find this proposal for one pastor per parish very attractive. However, those who have a passion to experience shared ministry, especially with the laity of the congregation, can experience this model as a most effective way to further that agenda.

Let me share with you a few of my experiences of being intentionally the only pastor in a congregation that had been, for nearly fifteen years, served by two pastors.

First, as the only pastor, authority and power has been focused. For the reasons discussed above, I believe this has been empowering to the ministry and has given the congregation courage to move forward. Most interestingly to me, the increased authority and power are rooted specifically in my being pastor and doing uniquely pastoral things. Specifically, my authority and power are located in preaching, presiding, and teaching. The congregation, because I have little choice but to be consumed with living one text at a time, expects and even demands that I, as their pastor, "speak Bible" and be explicitly evangelical. They are right in their perception that a significant amount of my time and energy is focused on biblical reflection for teaching and preaching. They would be surprised if that effort did not become actualized in bold proclamation, the asserting of a faithful vision, and in almost every conversation. The congregation would also be perplexed if the authority given to me was expressed apart from a biblical and theological framework. When I start to speak the language of psychology, business, or entertainment, their eyes begin to cross. I imagine them saying to themselves, "I wonder if he's preaching this week. He sure isn't consumed by the text like he usually is." Being the only pastor challenges me to insure a theological presence in the congregation. Be clear: I am not the only source of that presence, but if I fail to conserve the central theological foundation of the congregation, the congregation will be in danger of losing its soul. When I accept that I am (rightfully, I believe) authorized to be the pastoral leader, I am also held accountable in ways I would not otherwise be. When this happens, I find myself being held accountable not so much by the congregation, but by my ongoing biblical reflection, done in public, from which I cannot escape.

Being the only ordained minister in the congregation makes room for more involvement of the laity rather than less. In the congregation I serve as the only pastor, the above assertion is best illustrated in liturgy, pastoral care, and outreach ministry. The absence of more than one pastor means a cadre of assisting ministers exists to provide significant leadership for worship. Just as I wrestle with the text each week to preach, a member of the congregation engages the text in order to lead the congregation in prayer. Trained and authorized, these lay leaders share the ministry at the very core of our life together. The same is true for pastoral care. The congregation recognizes that I, as the only pastor, cannot provide the visitation for and keep company with *all* of those in need. For this reason, mobilizing and authoring a group of "pastoral partners" has become essential to the ministry. These people regularly visit and keep company with those who are homebound, in institutional settings, or are facing other significant transitions in their lives such as the birth of a child. One of these lay "pastoral partners," a police detective, said to me once, "I always wondered why you pastors got to have all the fun. Why didn't we get to visit and pray with people?"

The same happens in outreach ministry. Ministry from the congregation to the community has multiplied significantly because it does not, it cannot, flow through the pastor. The vacancy created when only one pastor serves a congregation creates the need and grants the authenticity to encourage and sustain these ministries. I am convinced that if there were more ordained pastoral staff, lay involvement would survive only as a token commitment to lay ministry rather than as a necessary and essential part of the congregational character. I believe much of this involvement happens because there is a sense that there is room for people to practice their faith. When talking about this, a member said, "I think that seeing Tim, Vicki, Nick, and Brian [assisting ministers] up front on Sunday encourages others to join in, like the swelling ranks in the choir, serving on committees, reading texts, teaching Sunday school, etc. It doesn't feel like participating in the service is reserved for the 'chosen few'. It's great."

Ordained pastors are expensive. Their extensive training, commitment to a lifestyle, and the responsibility they are given are appropriate reasons for commensurate financial compensation. However, the cost is not only the significant monetary expenditure. The more ordained clergy, the more institutional energy is consumed by these few and the less that energy is available for other staff.

I have found that putting together a staff team, made up of myself and other lay staff who have as their charge the formation of congregational character, removes the inevitable stratification that happens when some wear a collar and others do not. In any institution, the more levels or strata that exist, the more energy it takes to move the institution. With one pastor in the congregation instead of many, one significant level is eliminated. The formation of staff with one pastor affords opportunities that otherwise could not exist. A staff can be shaped to focus on the vision and direction of the congregation's call, not on specific positions.

For example, the congregation I presently serve has committed to move ever more deeply into and out of worship and attention to the primary symbols of Word and Sacrament. Their character develops through the practice of ritual integrity. Children have become a primary way for the congregation to embrace this mission. Inviting children into a consistent and accessible ritual practice gathers the whole congregation into this adventure. To embrace this mission, the staff team at Hope Lutheran includes myself (the only ordained pastor), a pastoral assistant who is a layperson with a theological degree in sacred music and liturgy, a youth and education director, and a parish administrator. The staff team has been formed to serve the congregation's vision. The ability to attract and sustain a team of such quality happens because those involved have a significant role in leading the congregation, not just in managing someone else's agenda (usually the pastor's). Even the mention of adding more ordained staff causes great anxiety among the team. Correctly, I believe, the staff fears the inevitable stratification that would happen with the presence of another ordained person.

Another way the congregation experiences inordinate expense from the presence of more than one ordained pastor is the common conflicts that arise in the relationships between pastors. The specific reasons for the conflicts are as numerous as the situations.

However, the fact that conflict is so prevalent among ordained pastoral teams indicates underlying systemic issues. One such issue might be that most pastors are trained as generalists. They are trained to preach, teach, and lead. In a staff with multiple ordained members, being a generalist is impossible. Sooner or later, the frustration of not fulfilling the call for which one was trained builds to the point of conflict. When conflict happens between pastoral leaders, the cost to the congregation and its mission is tremendous. Often, the fallout from such conflicts can wound the congregation's ministry for years, if not for decades. In addition, the pain and hurt experienced by the pastors thwarts their passion for the courageous leadership needed for effective ministry.

It would be very interesting to see what would happen if congregations chose to embrace a commitment to be served by one pastor. I imagine such an intentional practice would produce wondrous new questions and stir our imagination in ways we have not yet known.

Maybe, just maybe, the off-handed comment is right: "We do have too many pastors."

10

RECOVERING THE MINISTERIUM:
A CONGREGATION FOR PASTORS

The year is 2016. Pastor Stephens has been retired for a couple of years. He now spends most of his time being a member of a congregation he became involved in about seventeen years ago. Be clear: lest there be some misunderstanding, the congregation being talked about here is not the congregation Pastor Stephens served as pastor. No, this is a story about the particular community of faith that made it possible for Pastor Stephens to enjoy and be energized during the last years of his active ordained ministry. This story is about the power of the gospel that evangelized Pastor Stephens in and through a particular community of faith: the ministerium.

Seventeen years ago, at the close of the twentieth century, Pastor Stephens was not thrilled about being a pastor. Things were fine in the parish. There was no real conflict, no significant resistance to his leadership. He had just endured another congregational meeting without any real disasters taking place. Outwardly, things were going fine. But inwardly, Pastor Stephens was a mess. He hurt inside. It was as if his soul and his vocational commitment to being a pastor were under investigation by a special prosecutor. Every time he turned around, another piece of doubt and despair was uncovered. Some talked about it as burnout. Others spoke of the low morale among pastors. Still others just gave up and said that this was the way it was today for pastors. The only explanation for the situation was that pastors, like churches, had simply become insignificant and unnecessary. They existed only to keep alive a few nostalgic functions like baptisms, weddings, and funerals. His depression was just another example of how mainline churches had been sidelined. If it happened to congregations, it was only logical that it would happen to pastors as well.

Whatever it was, Pastor Stephens was no longer excited about being a pastor. In fact, there were days he was tempted to give it all up. A neighboring colleague had just resigned for no particular reason. Only in his early fifties, he had simply decided it wasn't worth it anymore. Such a bold and honest act, once seen as a sign of weakness, was now considered an act of honesty and courage. Almost every day Pastor Stephens wondered if he shouldn't be honest and muster the same courage.

It had not always been this way. Pastor Stephens remembered the early years of his ordained ministry. He had a sense of purpose and passion for who he was called to be and what he was called to do. He honestly felt like he made a difference. He was not just a cultural chaplain, but a necessary instrument of God in the task of unfolding a congregation, which in turn evangelized people, who in turn would be missionaries in the world. He preached with fervor and expected the gospel proclamation not to come back empty, but to really transform people. He prayed with intensity. He studied the Bible and read theology. He spent hours musing about esoteric theological ideas that he believed had some connection with the real life of the congregation. He argued with colleagues about eschatology, exegetical methodology, and homiletical approaches. He was alive and woke up each day ready to ride the roller coaster of ministry, encountering all the ups and downs with the confidence that God would keep him on the track. Sometimes his stomach would get caught in his throat. Other times he would scream out in terror. On many occasions, he would roar with laughter. There were days he would slowly climb to the top of the roller coaster track, ready for the freefall, trusting the track to hold him. But no matter what happened on the roller coaster of those early days of ministry, this much was true: he felt alive, honored, and thankful to be on the adventure of ordained ministry.

Now, more than twenty years after being set apart for the roller coaster of ordained ministry, the roller coaster had become a carousel that moved in boring circles, accompanied by gentle music, with only a slight lift—predictably up and down, again and again. Twenty years later, instead of a sleek roller coaster car, he was riding a beautifully crafted horsey, tame and domesticated by any standards. Worst of all, he had accepted this plight as the way it would be—the way it must be. And worse still, he hated the thought of riding in circles, saddle sore and bored, for another seventeen years until he retired. No wonder he admired his colleague who had dared to step off the horsey.

It was more than just a personal crisis; Pastor Stephens also despaired at what his internal struggle was doing to the congregation. Long ago, he had learned about "parallel process." He believed what was going on inside of him would inevitably be reflected in the life of the congregation. He wondered if the congregation wanted to quit, just like he wanted to quit. He wondered if congregational life was just another horsey ride for its members: people going in circles on the carousel of tamed and domesticated religious experience.

But then it happened. This is the story of how the last seventeen years of Pastor Stephens' ministry became a Lazarus story. As he looked back to seventeen years ago, his pastoral passion had been dead. He felt like he was Lazarus, all wrapped up tight in his death clothes, stinking to high heaven from death and decay. People grieved his passing and even asked God why it had to happen that such a promising pastoral life had to end so prematurely. Yet the miracle was that God, through Jesus, called him out of the tomb and back to life.

And God used the strangest of all means to make it happen. Or at least it seemed the most unlikely way an intervention would take place. Of all people, all institutions, it was the bishop who occasioned Pastor Stephens' redemption. It did not happen overnight. Yet he could remember when the tomb of his despair began to creep open.

Over the years, Pastor Stephens had become a bit cynical about bishops. Well, that's not true. He had become *very* cynical. He had become even more disillusioned about synodical gatherings like the annual synod assembly. It must have been God's wonderful sense of humor that the rebirth of Pastor Stephens began during the bishop's report at a synod assembly.

The bishop did the usual thank yous and acknowledgments at the beginning of the report, but then she was quiet for a moment. It was as if she were mustering up her courage. The silence was an anticipatory silence, like the hushed crowd just before the tightrope walker accepts the next, and most precarious, object to hold while balancing on the thin wire.

There was a sense of relief when she spoke, confidently and purposefully. "For the past year I have prayed, listened quietly for God's response, entered the biblical stories, and studied the traditions. I have been in dialogue with many of you, often without your knowing the questions through which I listened to your stories. I talked with the great teachers of the church and with other bishops. All the while, I have been haunted by a quixotic quest: 'How might the life-giving gospel of Jesus Christ embrace this world through the congregations of this synod?' I am tired of managing and attempting to fix real, but for the most part trivial, crises. Meetings, budgets, policies, and workshops leave me empty and weary. So I have decided to trade in my CEO role for a chance to fight windmills. I may look like the comic Don Quixote, naive and unrealistic, but the windmills must be engaged."

This was the strangest bishop's report anyone could remember. There was a stunned silence.

"All this became clear to me many months ago. God spoke to me in a most peculiar way—or maybe it was not all that unusual. You recall the tragedy experienced in the family of one our pastors, the devastating death of a child in an unfortunate accident. I was there, like many of you, to support and care for the pastor, his family, and the congregation. It was an honor to be asked to preach and preside at the funeral of that child. Following the worship service, while gathering in the church parlor for the continuation of the liturgy, one of you pulled me aside.

"It was clear that something important was on your mind. As this pastor began to speak with urgency, I was upset that even now he was asking me to fix some problem. I thought this was the case, because I knew the one who needed my ear was a pastor in the midst of significant conflict. The conflict was both internal and external. Internally, there was a real question about whether he had the energy, passion, and courage to continue to be an ordained minister. Externally, there were significant conflicts in the congregation. In other words, the pastor who pulled me aside could have been almost any one of you. He is a fairly normal pastor in our synod."

Muffled laughter arose from those assembled.

"I knew this pastor's story, so little needed to be said about the crises he was experiencing. Instead, he looked at me and said, 'This morning I met with my spiritual director. He asked me a strange question; he asked, 'Who is your pastor?' I stumbled around for a while, trying to figure out an appropriate answer to his question. Finally, I said clearly that it was my bishop. It was then I realized what I needed to pull me through these dark days. I needed a pastor who would preach the gospel, administer the sacraments, and gather a community of people together to challenge, support, and enlist me in the mission to which I have been called. Driving home from the meeting with my spiritual director, I remembered this gathering tonight."

The bishop took a sip of water and then continued on. "At this funeral luncheon, the pastor said to me, 'Bishop, I have a confession to make. I came to this funeral tonight not primarily because of my pastoral colleague and his deep anguish and hurt. I came because I needed my pastor. I needed to hear my pastor preach, and to receive the meal of grace and hope, and to be with my colleagues.'

"Then the pastor was silent for a moment, looked at me with tears in his eyes, and said, 'I have heard it said many times; now I repeat the proverbial saying that someone has to die before we, as pastors, get together.'"

The bishop stood silently looking at the assembly, and then with conviction and controlled passion, she spoke slowly and clearly so everyone would understand. "I declare to you today, it is time that we, the set-apart leaders of the church, get together around the one death that gives life. It is time I became the pastor of a congregation again and not just a bureaucrat. I realized at that funeral that I have been called to be a pastor to a congregation. The congregation I am called to serve is comprised of pastors, those set apart by lay ministry, church professionals, whoever else is set apart to lead, and the families of these leaders. Like most congregations, membership will be a bit ambiguous. But be clear: this congregation is comprised of leaders and their families who are set apart, formally or informally, to serve both a local congregation or ministry and the wider church.

"I am called to be their pastor, which means I will do what pastors do. I will preach the gospel of Jesus Christ as best I can. I will preside and administer the sacraments. I will teach. I will make pastoral visits. I will do all this as my first and top priority. Regular sacramental worship, teaching, and visitation will be what I will do.

"Such a commitment will involve significant changes in many areas, some of which I am sure I do not even know. But these changes will take place soon. I have conferred with the synod council and have their blessing. I did not ask for approval. Church councils do not approve a pastor's preaching, presiding, teaching, and visitation. But I did ask for feedback and blessing, for we are partners in this endeavor.

"Here are the immediate changes I foresee:

"One: I will regularly, at least every other week, and weekly whenever possible, preach, preside, and teach somewhere within the synod to a congregation of those set apart by evangelical leadership. This non-Sunday sabbath gathering will be focused on the intersection of the appointed texts and on being a set-apart leader of the church or the family member of such a leader. As in any congregation, it is assumed that those who are members will attend regularly. And, like any congregation, I know there will be inactive members as well. I am not asking pastors and others set apart for leadership and their families if they want to worship together and be embraced and held accountable to the gospel. I am stating that this is what pastors in this synod will do. I have been set apart to be your pastor. So I will do what pastors do. I will preach, preside, teach, and visit. I am your pastor. I will do what I am called to do!

"Two: I will not spend most of my time in local congregations as I am doing now. These congregations already have a pastor. Martin Luther claimed that the pastor was the bishop of the congregation, ministering to the priesthood of all believers. I will instead focus on the one congregation that does not, for all practical purposes, presently have a pastor: the group of those who are set apart for ministry, and their families. There is mission work to be done among these people. I have been called to that mission.

"Three: My important administrative responsibilities will flow out of the ministry of proclamation through Word and Sacrament. Refocusing my energy and time in this way will, I believe, both foster greater efficiency and make visible the many things that now consume so much time, energy, and resources, and provide so little benefit to the mission before us. Much of what I will not have time to do likely did not need doing.

"Four: I will enter this new mission field with the sense of adventure and urgency of a new mission developer. In many ways, this is what I imagine I will be doing: calling together a community of faith to embolden them for faithful witness and mission. Like most mission developers, this will be an act of faith. I am not sure what will happen. I only know that there is a cry I hear that I cannot silence. It is the cry of a significant group of people who want to, who need to, hear and experience the gospel of Jesus Christ through participation in a faithful community.

"Five: Finally, I begin this new call tomorrow. Tomorrow morning at 6:30 A.M., prior to breakfast and the beginning of our day's work as an assembly, there will be worship for those set apart for public ministry: pastors, associates in ministry, church professionals, and their families. I will preach and preside. I will claim my role as your pastor. Others of you, delegates who have been called to the important ministry of lay leadership within your congregation, are welcome to come. But do not be surprised when you hear preaching and prayers that focus on relating the texts to the world of the publicly set-apart leader."

The bishop was quiet for a moment, soaking in the stunned silence of the gathering. There was little reaction, mostly shock. What would this mean? Was it realistic? It felt as if, as a group, they wanted to chant in unison, "We've never done it this way before!"

Finally she spoke again, "I have intentionally announced this change in direction at an assembly with lay congregational leaders present. This is no secret movement or grab for power. It is no clever move toward a hierarchy. It is, however, an acknowledgment that those people the church has set apart to be its leaders have little opportunity to be encouraged, embraced, challenged, and provoked by the gospel of Jesus. Only the gospel can provide the challenge and encouragement that is needed.

"And further and most importantly, I trust and believe nothing will have a more transformative effect on local congregations than set-apart leaders who have heard, tasted, and been enveloped in the renewing power of the gospel. To say it another way, I trust I will better serve congregations of this synod by being a pastor to pastors and other set-apart leaders than I have been by being a CEO of the organization.

"So today I will begin my ministry as a mission developer. Tomorrow morning this new congregation will meet to worship. And I pray there will never be another pastor who comes to me and says, 'Isn't it a shame someone has to die in order for us to get together?' Unless, of course, this pastor is talking about our regular gathering in the name of the One who did die so that we might come together and be God's people. Thank you." And the bishop sat down.

That night a group of pastors gathered in the local bar for a few drinks and conversation. Pastor Stephens joined them. The discussion was lively. As usual, people began talking about the things they shared in common. Quickly moving past the weather, they spoke of movies. One of the group, John, had just rented the film *Life Is Beautiful* for the third time. John was known as a person who was always looking for something deep and rarely did anything just for the fun of it. He talked about how the movie was for him a parable of the gospel. The movie showed the power of imagining an alternative world in the midst of even the ugliest of oppressions: a concentration camp. John wondered aloud whether the playfully imaginative kingdom vision of Jesus might be the only hope for our world, so locked in destructive behavior.

When John had used up his obligatory five minutes of pontificating about something he thought was important, the conversation quickly changed to the bishop's pronouncement earlier in the day. Pastor Stephens listened as passions around the topic increased. Some were confused and did not know what the bishop was talking about. Someone jokingly said, "What has she been smoking?" Others thought they understood what she was saying but thought it was crazy, and the sooner they could convince her to give up this half-baked idea the better. Still others were frightened; they did not want to have the bishop be a pastor. They liked the present arrangement where the bishop stayed out of their lives unless they called. And besides, when would they find time to worship and pray and study? Was the bishop so out of touch that she had forgotten how busy they were doing ministry?

After a while, Don spoke up. He was one of those rare breeds among pastors who spoke only when he had something to say and when he had thought it through first. For this reason, when he spoke, the group paid attention.

"My concern," Don said carefully, "is that this really changes the role of the bishop. Whether we like it or not, the bishop's office has become primarily a human resource office for the church. They are primarily concerned about the working conditions of the employees, that is the pastors, and, to a much lesser degree, other church professionals. Mobility, conflict (almost always involving pastors in one way or another), discipline, and compensation are their focus. In addition, to the extent they can leverage their influence, the bishop's office has been concerned with job performance. Because they have no formal means of holding us accountable (except for "conduct unbecoming"), they must resort to such tactics as personal persuasion, teaching, workshops, and other forms of encouragement. As pastors, we have the final say about whether to avail ourselves of their services or not. It is not compulsory. In the present set up, the bishop is beholden to us."

Don was quiet for a moment, obviously collecting his thoughts. "It seems our bishop has decided to considerably downsize the human resource office and expend energy in another way. It seems she thinks she has authority from some place other than us. When she claims to be our pastor, she sounds as if she wants to do more than influence us. She expects to lead us in the name of God. I am not sure what all this means, but if it happens, things will be different for us. To use the language of business, she is really thinking 'outside the box.' We had better pay attention to this. I have a sense that this could really change our lives as pastors."

Then the conversation got really heated. Some said they should stop their bishop right away. It was proposed that maybe they should boycott the worship service the next morning. If only a few showed up, the bishop would get the point. However, for a group of people who prided themselves on their church-personship, this was a difficult tactic to support. Yet maybe, just maybe, sometimes you had to do really difficult things to get your point across.

The evening conversation ended as most such discussions do. No clear decision was made. Pastor Stephens went back to his room tired and confused after a long day. He was even more exhausted when he considered that tomorrow morning at 6:30 he was supposed to attend a worship service and join a congregation.

Lying in bed, he tried to read, but he couldn't concentrate. Just before he nodded off to sleep, he thought about John's comments about the movie *Life Is Beautiful*. Sometimes it felt that life as a pastor was anything but beautiful. His life was no concentration camp, to be sure, but there were moments, ever-increasing moments, when he felt imprisoned in his call to be a pastor. Maybe, like the main character in the movie, the bishop was trying to imagine an alternative world, a way of experiencing beauty in the midst of difficult times. He recalled how his liturgics professor once taught him that liturgy was "making believe." Liturgy was "kingdom play," acting out an alternative vision for living. Was this what the bishop was trying to offer them? Through the power of liturgy, was the bishop inviting him to "make believe" and get involved in "kingdom play"? Before Pastor Stephens went to sleep, he made sure the alarm was set so he would not miss the 6:30 A.M. worship service.

The next morning, without Pastor Stephens knowing it, the tomb was beginning to open on his despair. Attending the 6:30 A.M. worship service was the beginning of getting off the carousel and moving toward the roller coaster. Now, seventeen years later, a newly retired pastor, he knows what he could not have known then: when he was brought into a community of faith gathered around Word and Sacrament, he again began to enjoy, in the deepest way, being a pastor.

The bishop's commitment was not easy for her to keep or for others to accept. There was significant resistance to this change. The bishop was attacked from all sides. Some local congregations felt betrayed (although it was interesting that these congregations were often served by pastors who detested the idea of a worshiping ministerium). A few pastors were public and vocal in their refusal to be involved, and many more participated minimally. It was also known that other bishops and the churchwide offices were leery of her approach to being a bishop. Sometimes her commitment to being a pastor to the ministerium meant that she was unable to perform the bureaucratic tasks assigned her. Although she never spoke of this friction, its presence was known throughout the synod. The bishop and her synod were known for her maverick activities. The synod was like a troubled child, endured and tolerated, but a source of great discomfort and unease.

However, the bishop remained committed to this mission. Soon she was leading worship almost every week in one part of the synod or another. She was organizing the rest of her work around these gatherings. Most of the services were in the evening and included a meal and a time for education. She tried to order these gathering much like a normal congregation's Sunday gathering. Soon, a ministry to the children of set-apart leaders was developed in some settings.

Pastor Stephens and his family attended almost every ministerium gathering they could. They would travel a couple of hours to join in this time that focused around worship but included education and fellowship. Soon he began to place these events on his local church calendar and was bold about telling the congregation he served how important it was for him to be with his pastor, the bishop, and his congregation. At first, the congregation he served was a bit put off by this. They had never had to share their pastor in this way before. But soon, as they saw him being renewed and encouraged in his ministry, and saw that it enhanced his presence to and with them, they accepted it, and some even insisted he attend.

When the ministerium worship was in the area where Pastor Stephens served, he was notified of this and asked if he desired a pastoral visit from the bishop. On other occasions he was called and informed—not asked, but informed—that the bishop would like to stop by for a visit. More than once this visit involved not just him, but his wife and even his family.

A couple years after initiating this approach, the bishop was up for reelection. There was a strong movement to defeat her and return to the old ways of doing things. The opposition forces, in a rare overtly political move, put forth an opposition candidate. Maybe it was her continual preaching and public prayer life and the courage this gave her; or maybe it was her personal strength and character; or maybe (and this is what Pastor Stephens believed) it was the Spirit of God working in and through her. Whatever it was, she did not back away from her vision. In fact, she entered it more deeply. As she spoke to the assembly about her vision for the future, she talked of a new way of staffing the bishop's office. She wanted to have fewer staff people, but she wanted to ensure that there would be one assistant to the bishop whose responsibility it would be to attend to the ritual life of the synod. She spoke of new ways to support families, including a family camp at one of the Bible camps for set-apart leaders and their families. She talked of doing all they could to have those involved in the candidacy process be connected to the ministerium. She spoke of just beginning to learn how to be a pastor to this congregation of set-apart leaders.

The atmosphere around the election was charged with energy. There was a clear choice. Although the rhetoric was passionate, the present bishop was easily reelected, and the vision she claimed was affirmed. The synod had made the choice to venture more deeply into a new way of understanding and organizing itself. Some called it moving away from a bureaucratic practice to a liturgical practice of being a synod. Some just said this bishop made it enjoyable and meaningful to be a leader in the church.

Pastor Stephens watched as all this developed. From his perspective, not without bias, to be sure, for he was a strong advocate

of the bishop and her vision, it seemed that congregational conflict lessened, collegiality increased, and competitiveness diminished. When he regularly gathered around the table of the Lord
with his brothers and sisters set apart for public ministry, when he
confessed to and with them, when he prayed for and with them,
somehow he could not so easily separate from them.

It was not always easy. He did not particularly care for some
fellow pastors. He disagreed passionately with some about one
issue or another. Yet, since they worshiped together regularly, he
embraced them as people to whom he was connected through
Jesus Christ. Interestingly, there was an increased amount of
support and connection between the synod and congregations.
As trust between the bishop and those set apart to lead congregations grew (and this happened because the bishop fostered
trust by being—through preaching, presiding, and teaching—
open, honest, predictable, and respectful), there was excitement
and joy in participating in the life of the broader church. Also,
because their contact with the bishop, which was regular and
consistent, was mediated through Word and Sacrament, they
found they were drawn to the continual challenge and support
that was part of their life. She had an authenticity that had been
unavailable to her when she had grounded her authority in
bureaucratic functions.

The more the synod lived a liturgical understanding of its
life, the more it imagined alternative ways to encourage leaders. Book clubs grew. One of the most fascinating was a book
club for those members of the ministerium who were in high
school. A mission trip was planned for members of the ministerium and their families. A choir was formed. Late each summer a picnic was held that included a liturgy of sending
(designed by the new synod staff person who was responsible
for the ritual life of the synod) for children going off to kinder-
garten and college. Baby showers, weddings, and more became
commonplace.

There was much discussion when one of the young pastors asked the bishop to baptize her daughter at one of the ministerium worship services. The bishop agreed, and during the education time following that worship, the community talked about how the children of those set apart to be leaders must live out their baptism in Christ with the demands of being part of a family that was a public presence. This imposition on their lives demanded a community of support. Local congregations could not give that support. The ministerium had that potential. Some thought baptism in the context of the ministerium started the church down the slippery slope of claiming a qualitative difference in the sacrament for lay people and for pastors.

The conversation was amazing and insightful. On the way home, Pastor Stephens realized that such a conversation would never have happened in the old bureaucratic system. Someone might have written a resolution for the assembly, or seminary professors might have written arguments about why one perspective was more appropriate than another. But now, a community of faith was wrestling with its life together. He whispered over the sound of the car radio, "It is sure great to be a pastor."

The joy of being a leader in the church was shared by many in the synod. This excitement and commitment to mission and ministry was infectious. Congregations were led into new and daring ministries. Conflict was present, but more often than not it was over something worth fighting about. And, because the pastor and other leaders had support outside their congregations, they were less reactive, and conflict became not an emotional battlefield, but an opportunity for movement and courageous mission. It seemed that the more active the set-apart leaders of a congregation were in the ministerium, the more boldly the congregation engaged in evangelical witness and mission.

Pastor Stephens was still involved in active ministry when the election of another bishop took place. By now, the synod's character was shaped by this new understanding of its life together.

Those leaders who found this approach oppressive had left for other synods that functioned in the old bureaucratic way. Those who came into the synod knew the context in which they would be providing evangelical leadership. The election of the new bishop involved first discerning where God was calling the synod, and most specifically the congregation of the ministerium. Then, and only then, could they seek out the leader who would challenge them into that vision. What amazed some of the old-time pastors like Pastor Stephens was that potential bishop candidates were considered based on their ability to preach, preside, and teach. Pastor Stephens could remember when bishops were elected based on their perceived ability to be administrators, pastoral care providers, or, although this was rarely stated, how well they could act busy and stay out of the life of pastors and congregations. As the election unfolded, Pastor Stephens realized he was now living his life as a pastor in a radically new way.

Now retired, Pastor Stephens is still involved in the ministerium. Rarely does he miss the weekly gathering. In fact, he and his wife are greeters and are on the list to make communion bread. They have made themselves available to provide child care for some of the younger pastors and leaders in the area; they love being a surrogate grandma and grandpa. Their personal devotions include praying the membership list, fluid as it is, for those in the ministerium. They also make calls on widows and widowers from the ministerium congregation.

On vacation once, Pastor Stephens and his wife visited a seminary classmate, recently retired from a congregation in another synod. As they talked, their old friend spoke of how hard it was for him to leave the congregation he had served for many years. The congregation had been his whole life. Leaving seemed even harder on his wife, for the only friends she had were in the congregation. Now they felt so alone, so forgotten, and so empty. They had joined another congregation in town, but it was not the same. This pastor said, "Being an active parish pastor was lonely enough, but being a retired pastor is like being a nobody."

The next time Pastor Stephens gathered with the ministerium congregation, he remembered this old seminary friend, and he was thankful that he was not alone during his ministry. During his retirement, it did not feel as if he had left his congregation. Now he and his wife have more time to invest in the congregation to which he really belonged, the ministerium. During coffee, he told some fellow congregants, "As long as I gather with you brothers and sisters, as long as we are called together around Word and Sacrament by one who has been set aside to be our leader, as long as I belong to this congregation that is committed to being the body of Christ, I am somebody. Nobody can take this away from me." Then he lifted his coffee cup, as if it were a goblet prepared for a toast at a great feast, and said, "Isn't it a great honor and joy to be a leader in the church?"

PART FOUR
CHRISTIAN COMMUNITIES OF THE FUTURE

11

FAITHFUL COMMUNITY: A CREATION MYTH

They sat on the rock, high on the ridge that rimmed the valley below. As usual, Thomas picked up little rocks and threw them over the edge. His father watched them fall. Together they had thrown many stones over this cliff. They had hiked this trail often in recent years and normally stopped here to look at the town, their town, below. Looking down at their home and throwing rocks invited Thomas to think seriously and ask questions.

Thomas, now in high school, still had the habit of rubbing his ear thoughtfully and throwing a rock as far as he could just before he asked his father one of his serious questions, which often were phrased, "How did this or that come to be?"[1] When Thomas asked questions like this, his father called them *creation questions*. By this the father meant that they were deep questions that demanded thoughtful responses. Thomas posed his questions this way because he had learned the kind of answer he would receive from his father. His father was a wise man. He did not speak frivolously. His words were chosen carefully, like the footsteps on the slippery path that led to this view of the world. Usually, once Thomas asked the question, his father would sit quietly for a while and throw a few stones, as if his father's stones

117

were chasing the ones Thomas had already thrown; then he would respond, "A good question. That will take some thought." When Thomas's father responded like this, Thomas smiled, for it meant they would take another hike.

The answer to the question was normally a story. The story was filled with verifiable data and rooted in rational, learned, and scientific study. But the answer, in that it was an answer at all, was much more than that; for the facts and figures, the data and science, the verifiability only provided the barest outline. It was the story told in, around, and through this material that revealed a truth. If Thomas listened carefully, he could sense the power embedded in these stories.[2] If he drifted off or started watching the birds in the air or the ground squirrel on the rocks, he usually got lost and confused. Thomas learned that once he strayed from the path of listening, finding the way back on course was hard work.

So on this day, seated on the ridge overlooking the valley that held their hometown, Thomas asked, pointing to the church steeple on the edge of town, "How did the church come to be?"

The father thought a moment and then asked, "Are you asking about how people come to be Christians?"

"No," Thomas replied.

"Are you asking about how that building was built?"

"No."

Thomas's father was quiet for a long time, so Thomas again asked, "How did they—the group of people who call themselves Christians and belong to the church—how did they come to be?"

"Oh," said his father, "that is a big question. That is *the* big question."

The next weekend they packed a backpack for their hike: a few sandwiches, some cookies, water bottles, the usual. And they packed a book. The son recognized it as the Bible.

Before long they were sitting quietly on their stone throne, surveying the vista before them. The silence was broken by Thomas, who asked, pointing to the steeple below, "How, then, did it come to be? How did God's people come to be?"

His father unzipped the backpack and took out the book. Then he said, "The answer to your question is here. This book, the Bible, is the story of the forming of a people. It is told in many and various ways. It is not a book of facts and figures. Scientific methods and modern principles of history may find it flawed. Yet the group of people who live this story find it to be a story that gives them identity and mission and meaning."[3]

"Before I try to tell the story," his father continued, "remember these three things. First and foremost, the main character in this story is a God who calls this people into being and who promises they will never be outside of God's love and care. Second, remember God is most interested in shaping a people, not in renewing individuals. God works in and through community. In fact, as you will hear, God is a community.[4] Lastly, remember that this people, created by God and formed into a community, has a mission. They are sent to be witnesses to God's unending love for all creation. Three things to remember: God called a people, and he gathered them into a community. This community has a mission: it exists for others."

The father reached into the backpack, took out a water bottle and a couple of cookies, and handed them to the son. "You might want to get comfortable; this is a long story."

The father told a story—a true story, to be sure—but told in his own words. Scientists and historians may have found this story flawed, but the father's telling revealed its deep truth and power. It bore the deep marks of the biblical story that continues to unfold even today. The father told a story of the creation, and the ongoing creating, of God's people. Thomas listened closely as his father told how God created community and revealed its mission. He did not get distracted, and he easily entered into the story, finding its truth and power.

∽

Word! A spoken word moved over chaos and brought forth a people. *Word!* An alien Word from outside, from beyond, from some other sphere, it implied a relationship, a hearing, an other who would respond. *Word!* God spoke and in this Word, which is breath with meaning, God's Spirit settled upon all that was and "called, gathered, and enlightened and made holy the whole Christian church,"[5] a holy people. It began and it has continued with *Word!*

To grasp how God's chosen people came to be, you must open your ears to Word. God speaks and births a people. God speaks and forms relationships. God speaks and calls a people to mission. This people is forever shaped and formed by God's speaking Word.

Yet, be clear, this Word of God is no set of propositions. Word cannot be tied down and defined. Word breaks into this world and calls forth new creation, especially the creation of a people, of imagination and openness. Word is more poetry than prose, more dream than definition, more art than science. Word opens the future to newness and does not close the door on possibility. Word will always create.[6]

God's people are a people of Word.

Yet early on the people began to distort this Word. They saw not an imaginative invitation to embrace the future; rather, Word was seen as a threat to the people's own construction of reality. Soon the people sought to take responsibility for their own lives, to become speakers of their own words. They sought to create their own peoplehood by asserting a proposition of what was right and wrong rather than surrendering and living in relationship with God.[7] In trusting their own words, the people did not and could not hear God's Word. This is sin—to trust any word other than God's Word.

The story of God's people, even as it is lived today, is the story of a people more often than not deaf to Word and much too eager to trust their own words. But it is also the story of a God who will not stop speaking Word, a God whose passion, love, imagination, and grace compel ongoing re-creation of a people. It is the story of a God whose breath will not be stopped and whose mission it is to include all creation, now divided and in the death throes of sin, in the embrace of Word.

Early in this story of God's people, God forcefully and dramatically reveals two options. Be open to Word and know life, or trust your own words and know death. The stories of Adam and Eve and the fall in the Garden of Eden, of Cain and Abel, and of the Tower of Babel are stories of the choice that faced God's people: God's Word or their own words.

In the face of this forced choice, God's people fell to the temptation to turn Word from being a source of imagination, openness, and newness to its opposite. The people saw Word as a set of rules, teachings, and instructions. Too often they used it to ensure perfection and rightness, rather than imagination and ongoing creation. Word was used to shut the windows on the wind of spirit and to foster the illusion of stability and strength. This use of Word finally drove God to such despair that God again spoke Word, this time to bring forth chaos out of creation, a flood, drowning the rigid order created by the people. This nearly destroyed all God had created.

Yet God knew that with no creation, no people, no one to hear, there would be no Word. For Word is Word only when it is heard and received. God is a God of Word, and so God repented. A rainbow reminder challenged the God of Word to imagine (this is what Word does!) another way to unfold a people. The God of Word had to set aside dualistic ways of speaking. The temptation to think over and against, right and wrong, is too great in a closed system. Word brings to life imagination and an openness that can't exist in a closed system.

So begins a long journey. Abraham and Sarah left their settled ways and became the parents of a people and nation, for God spoke and called them forth on a journey that began with an encounter with Word.

The journey was marked by trust, wrestling, doubt, and disappointment. Word, always so vulnerable and so soon silenced, struggled to hold the faith and imagination of Abraham and Sarah in place. The daring imagination of promise that would be fulfilled called forth a whole people who passed Word on from generation to generation. Isaac, Abraham and Sarah's laughter child (for he was beyond hope), gave birth to Jacob, the grabber. Jacob did not play by the rules yet creatively imagined how to boldly embrace a future. Even God was fair game in this wrestling match, and Jacob grabbed God's blessing along with everything else and limped away into a future of possibility. Through Isaac and Jacob, Word began to break out of the polar boundaries of right and wrong, good and bad. God, through Word, shaped a people who envisioned the world differently.

Later, in Joseph's story, God's presence (even God's very name) remained quiet until the end. It was as if God and Word had been sent to slavery along with Joseph. Finally, after bringing his family to Egypt and to the supposed safety of a rich land, Joseph envisioned a new truth. Joseph said to those who had wronged him and sold him into slavery that they must see in new ways. They must understand that what they had meant for evil, God had turned to good. Word again sustained a people out of chaos into creation, out of a closed system into imagination.

The stories of the patriarchs and matriarchs provided an adventure into a different way to be a people. In these stories, Word again challenges and dismisses the dualism of right and wrong, good and bad, those in and those out. In light of these foundational stories, God's people must think of themselves in a new way.

∽

Thomas, taking a sip of water, looked at the church steeple. He recalled the stories he had learned in Sunday school. He never did understand certain stories, like God demanding that Abraham sacrifice Isaac, only to back down at the last moment.[8] Or the story of Jacob cheating his brother Esau. Or Joseph's brothers being mean and deceitful and then being forgiven. These stories seemed to give permission for wrong to triumph over right; for good to be silenced by bad. Thomas said to his father, "I don't get it. Wouldn't the people of God be really confused by these stories? What kind of God, what kind of church, would live by stories like this? A God beyond right and wrong? It doesn't make sense."

"You're right," the father said as he handed his son a cookie. "It's hard work to understand God. But the stories don't lie." Then the father continued.

~

Word brings creation out of chaos. So it was in Egypt. The people of Abraham and Sarah, the generations that followed Jacob and Joseph, the people of God, became slaves in Egypt. Burdened by oppression, the Hebrew people could only faintly hear the echo of Word.

Yet Word again cried out. Responding to the anguished lament of the people, Word called forth a new possibility. A reluctant leader, Moses, sent by God, spoke Word to the power of Pharaoh and said, "Let my people go." Word plagued the land and people of Egypt. Pharaoh, who could not hear Word and thus faced death, in desperation finally set free God's people who had been passed over by the angel of death.

Again it happened: a people created by Word out of chaos. This people was led into the wilderness, through the waters of the sea, and into freedom. Word creates a community open to freedom.

In the wilderness, wandering and led by Word now revealed in a pillar of cloud and fire, in manna and quail, in tablets of stone that announced a covenant, and in a promise of a land, Word taught a new way to be community. On the far side of the Red Sea, God's people began the unending process of being shaped and thus claiming a distinctive character as God's chosen people.

~

Thomas looked down on the town below. He looked at the church steeple and appreciated in a new way how different the church looked from all the other buildings. It was distinctive. The building seemed to say, "This is a peculiar place for a peculiar people."

Thomas asked his father, "How are God's people different?"

The sun was falling behind them, and it was time to begin their walk home. The father stood up, stretched, and said, "Let's start home. As we walk, we can consider your question." Stepping carefully as shadows emerged, the father spoke, at first quickly reviewing where they had been.

∽

The Word's presence with Abraham and Sarah and those that followed began to chip away at the dualistic, right-and-wrong view of community. God worked in and through scoundrels and cheats. Word used what was bad for good. A view of the world that divided life into two neat arenas could no longer exist. People were confused, but in that confusion they learned to see themselves differently.

In the wilderness, God revealed a vision of community that held three characteristics in tension rather than two. The struggle, a struggle that continues today, is for God's people to let go of the neatly ordered world of right and wrong, in and out, and instead be called into a life of movement, juggling, and tension. The dynamics of *three* replace the static ways of *two*.

What the people of God learned in the wilderness was the trauma, wonder, danger, and great joy of surrendering their compulsive way of envisioning life as having clear boundaries and certainty. Instead, Word called them forth to embrace life as an ever-dynamic journey of trust and faith. The people of God became a peculiar people when they were taught to live in this triadic notion of faithful community.[9]

∽

As they hiked down the hill, the father looked intently at his son and then at the church below. He wanted to be sure Thomas understood. So much of the world, and even so much of the church, seemed to contradict this notion. The father wondered how he could help his son, who would soon be venturing out on his own, to grasp this important truth. He did not know how he could do this. But something inside him told him it must be done.

As the day ended, Thomas's father said, "This is what makes God's people peculiar: they are a people whose identity is a dynamic tension between three, not two, but three characteristics. In the wilderness, God's people began to live this tension. On our next hike, I will tell you about the wilderness."

A week later, they took a breakfast hike. Early morning hikes had become rarer as Thomas had gotten older. Thomas loved sleeping in on Saturdays. But this Saturday, if there was going to be a hike, it had to be early; Thomas had an afternoon commitment to complete an English project with two other students. Each of them had been studying one aspect of a Shakespeare play. Today they would put their work together for the class presentation. In fact, it was Thomas's English project that triggered how his father would explain the wilderness.

The two of them perched on the ledge, looking east and watching the sun rise and a new day begin. They sipped hot, strong coffee, a newly discovered treat for Thomas, and feasted on bagels.

Thomas rubbed his ear and said, "How, then, did the wilderness make the people peculiar?"

Thomas's father had been waiting for the question.

∽

The wilderness journey was a classroom.[10] The lessons learned, the character that emerged forged not only the head, but also the heart, the hands, and the feet of God's people. The wilderness school not only taught concepts but demanded that the people live out the triadic, threefold character that was being taught. First, the wilderness was a place of radical dependence on the

God of Word, a dependence marked by a response of *praise*. Second, Word provided instructions for living and structuring life so that it could be experienced fully. The focus of this is *righteousness*. Third, the people were challenged not to forget that the Word called them to side with the poor, the outcast, the stranger, and the forgotten. This preference compelled God's people to profound acts of *compassion*.

How did God's people come to be, and how do they continue to come to be? The answer is that Word shaped them into a people who would hold these three elements in dynamic tension. Like a juggler, they could not focus on only one and let the others fall. They must keep up the unending challenge to hold three together at once; continually reaching, searching, letting go, and grasping again. Only then would they be what the God of Word called them to be.

～

The father saw a confused look on Thomas's face, so he told Thomas to imagine a project for the wilderness school. Each of three students must research one part of the triadic notion of faithful community. One would explore praise, another righteousness, and the other compassion.

"Now," the father said, excited about finding a way to clarify the confusion, "imagine the presentation done by the wilderness school student who focused on praise. It might have gone like this."

The father took out a party hat from his backpack and pretended to be a wilderness school student standing before the class.

～

Look! Imagine that down below us is a small sea. Miraculously, we have been led through the sea on dry land. Now we stand on the far banks. Only moments before we had seen the approach of Pharaoh's army, the dust from the desert floor rising like a cloud in the distance. They are coming closer and soon, so it seems, our freedom will end.

But look again! Now in the sea there is a churning of water. For the dry land, our pathway through the waters from death to life, now holds Pharaoh's army in bondage. We are free, and he is bound. Life is victorious, and death is swallowed up in the sea below.

We are God's people. Led by Moses, who Word called to be our leader, we have been freed and now are part of the wilderness school. The first lesson taught to us happened naturally and immediately. Gazing below, what else could we do: we danced and sang and offered praise to the One who had set us free!

> I will sing unto the Lord
> For God has triumphed gloriously,
> The horse and rider thrown into the sea (kersplash).
>
> The Lord my God,
> My strength, my song,
> Has now become my victory.
>
> The Lord is God and I will praise him
> The Father's God and I will exalt him.[11]

∽

Thomas joined in singing the song with his father. He had learned it years before as a child at Bible camp.

When they finished, they laughed. Then Thomas's father continued as if he were still the wilderness school student.

∽

We sang; our feet began to dance, we clapped, and we felt alive like never before. Our dancing, our singing, and our celebration gave us the gift of being a people. Praise united us and gave us an identity. The praise we sang and danced and clapped was praise not for ourselves; it was the God of Word who brought us out of bondage into freedom. This was not our strategic plan, or the disciplined application of goals and objectives, or even "thinking outside the box." God broke into our world as God always has, from the outside, with Word. When we were trapped in bondage, Word granted us what we could not imagine on our own: a new creation as a free and saved people.

In response to this extraordinary gift of life, freely given, God's people are forever marked as a people of praise. Yet this praise is not just a response to what has been done; it shapes the future character of the people, because we know this Word will not stop granting the gift.

∽

Thomas's father took off the party hat and pulled out a hard hat from the backpack.

"Now it is time for the second presentation. I am now the wilderness school student who will explain righteousness to you," the father said.

∽

Oh, it was fun practicing praise! Yet sooner or later, we got hungry and tired and afraid of the dark. Some began to complain. Praise alone left us empty and vulnerable to the dangers of the wilderness. How would we eat? Where would we go? What would we do? What kind of life would we live?

Some of us were so afraid of freedom, so anxious about the unknown, that we even looked longingly back to Egypt and slavery. "Better to be slaves and have some structure than to be free and die."

Chaos. Again chaos. And again God came to us through Word.

God heard our cries. Word, which brought order to chaos, now took many shapes. Word entered our life through practical instruments that granted us a way to live the wonderful gift of freedom we had been given.

Word became a cloud by day and a pillar of fire by night to lead us on our wilderness wanderings. Word became manna and quail so we might be fed and nourished as we meandered through the desert. Word became a covenant, carved in tablets of stone, so we might know the elements of the relationship that must receive constant and vigilant attention. Word sent us leaders who provided organization.

God had set us free, but God did not stop there. God did not abandon us to anarchy and an existence without boundaries. God sent Word. The order and structure given us reflected the God who called us into being. Praise echoed constantly through our lives. We continually tapped our feet and whistled the song. The God who calls us into being and provokes us to praise is the same God who leads and guides us through life. God, by giving order and structure, names us a righteous people.

Word, providing order, structure, and administration for the community, offers the second characteristic of God's faithful people: the characteristic of righteousness. Righteousness is the right ordering, structuring, and administration of the community. God, in God's great wisdom, calls us to be a people who attend to the practical realities of how to live out the gift of life we have been given.

◦◦

The father looked at his son and decided it was time to move around a bit. He took off the hard hat and said, "There is more to be told, but let's take a walk." He fished two candy bars out of the backpack. He also took out a head lamp that they used for night hikes. Thomas wondered what it was for; he could see that his father had planned all this and was having fun. Thomas smiled as he let his father pull him up and lead them on the walk. As they walked, Thomas's father spoke.

"Two characteristics are made known. Yet, when there are two, a battle wages. Some could see the righteousness of providing structure and order as bondage and a threat to freedom. Some could see exuberant praise as anarchy and as a threat to being practical and getting work done. The lines could be drawn. Some are in, and some are out. Relationships are then severed. God would be perceived as choosing one side or the other. Again, this dualistic view of life could lead to yet another kind of chaos, but to this chaos again came Word. God entered the chaos, not by drawing lines and bringing clarity, but by sending Word to make the crisis even more complex. Add another characteristic, and the choosing of sides would be mitigated. Word challenged the people of God to imagine yet another element to hold in tension and to provide imaginative confusion, overwhelming the inevitable false certainty of one against another.

"Word called the people of God to set aside the temptation to strike a triumphant posture, even though they were named and claimed as God's people (praise) and ordered their life in light of that reality (righteousness). Word challenged the people to be a community of radical compassion."

Then Thomas watched as his father put the light on a headband and turned on the light. It was the middle of the morning. His father looked as strange as he did wearing the party hat or the hard hat.

Now in character, he was the third wilderness school student.

∽

Over and over as we wandered in the wilderness, Word broke into our life and reminded us, "Remember, you were once slaves in Egypt!" This memory, which we so easily forgot, held the seed of the characteristic of compassion. God had heard our cries as slaves in Egypt. God acted for our sake. God did not side with the powerful, the mighty, the pharaohs of this world. We were poor and forsaken, yet God heard our anguished and desperate cries, and God responded.

Word shattered our inevitable temptation to turn inward. Word refused to allow us to focus on ourselves by continually reminding us that the God who called us into being has a special preference for the poor, the outcast, the forsaken, the stranger, and the enemy. We must continually attend to those who are outside our boundaries, whether those boundaries be physical, emotional, political, or even spiritual.

Listen carefully. God does not prefer those who cry out in anguish because of anything they do or are. God does not look with favor upon the lowly and thus cause lowliness to become a virtue in and of itself. God's care for the poor is not for the sake of describing the virtues of the poor. Rather, God's commitment boldly asserts a characteristic of God. God hears the cries of those who are broken and empty, and this openness to those who are silenced and forgotten announces God's deep and abiding compassion.

Word thus comes again and again and reminds us that the God who called us into being is a God of compassion. And this God challenges us to practice the dangerous and vulnerable act of inviting into the core of our being those who are poor, forgotten, and forsaken, even those who are enemies. Word challenges the community of faith to always open its ears, its hands and arms, and its heart and mind to the least of these.

~

They had walked back to the perch from which they had started. Thomas's father found a weather-beaten scrub tree with three nubs near the top. He placed each of the hats on one of the nubs. As he placed each one, he spoke its name: praise, righteousness, compassion. They both laughed at the confused scarecrow look of the tree.

Then Thomas's father said, "The wilderness school taught God's people that they must learn to wear all three hats. When they do, they will certainly be a peculiar people."

It was now late morning, and it would soon be time to walk back down the hill. For a while they sat in silence, collecting their thoughts. Then, as if cued by some outside force, they both stood up and began the hike home. For a while they walked quietly. Then Thomas, tentatively at first, began to put together what he had heard today and in the weeks before.

૮ઌ

God's Word calls God's people into being and into a relationship. God wants to bring together all creation in a community of hope and joy. This mission continues today.

Word creates community out of nothing. The community responds with praise. Yet praise is not just a response; it also unfolds the character of a people. Praise responds to the past and anticipates a future.

Word, God's Word, does not only create community; it structures the gift of life that the community has been given. When God's people practice righteousness, they make the community work. Through righteousness, Word grants guidance and instruction for how to live out the gift that has been given so freely.

૮ઌ

Thomas was on a roll. His father laughed to himself. His son always could say everything more clearly than his father could.

Thomas did not notice his father's pride, but he continued on.

૮ઌ

Finally, Word won't allow the community to polarize around praise and righteousness. Instead, Word reminds God's people of a third characteristic to hold in tension with the other two. God's people, in that they reflect the God who called them into being and are crafted by Word, are a people of compassion. They must not be so caught up in their own freedom (praise) or their own structures and orderings (righteousness) that they close their ears and hearts to the most vulnerable and broken (compassion).

૮ઌ

Thomas finished and unconsciously reached down and picked up three stones. Instead of throwing them as he usually did, Thomas juggled the three. Often, one of the stones would fall when he lost his focus on the movement of the three and attended to only one or two of them in isolation. When one fell, he reached down, picked it up, and began to juggle again.

His father watched and smiled. He said nothing, for the continual dynamic movement of the stones, held together by some mysterious energy, said all that was needed.

∽

It was a couple of weeks before they could again go on a hike and talk. The walk was occasioned by another of the son's questions. "How did it come to be that the church, our church, has lasted so long? How did a Word-shaped people, taught in the wilderness school, survive all these years? Who kept the Word alive?"

As usual they packed a lunch, some water, and candy. In addition, the father threw a Bible into the pack. Off they went. They sat on their rock and looked out upon the town below. Then the father took out the Bible and began to speak.

∽

God is a God of Word. Word makes possible a relationship, a coming together, a speaking and a listening. Word reveals God's deep and abiding passion for relationships.

The Old Testament is a story of God's Word dwelling among the people. The Old Testament is a course of study, a curriculum.[12] The stories describe a people who struggle to live out what they learned in the wilderness. As God's people wrestled with how to juggle the three characteristics of praise, righteousness, and compassion, they often became weary. They would settle into one of the characteristics and claim it as the whole truth. When this happened, God would again speak Word and remind the people of the dynamic character that was central to their lives.

So it happened that priests got too caught up in praise and forgot about righteousness or compassion. God would send prophets and kings who, using Word, reminded the people of

God's whole vision and brought the people back to their juggling of the three characteristics.

Or sometimes, judges and kings would become anxious and afraid. They sought to create, protect, and defend people using their own techniques, power, and wisdom. They became so consumed with the pragmatic aspects of ordering a people that they forgot about God and the poor. So God sent priests and prophets who, through Word, would remind even the most powerful that their role was but a part of the whole, and that God and the poor must not be forsaken, even at the altar of being efficient, practical, or prudent. Praise and compassion must not be tossed aside in response to the need for good order and practice.

Sometimes the people of God became so open to the outsider that their posture of compassion led to accommodation with the world around them. Their openness to the stranger, and even the enemy, led to their losing their own identity. So God would send priests and kings who, through Word, would remind the people of who and whose they were. They must not be so open that they would lose their identity. Praise and righteousness must provide boundaries to the compassion to which the people were called.

The Old Testament is a story of God's people continually being shaped by Word and invited to juggle the three characteristics of praise, righteousness, and compassion. Faithfulness to this vision of community demands holding these three characteristics in a dynamic tension. Unfaithfulness means resolving the tension and settling on one or two of the characteristics to the exclusion of the others.

༄

The father found three stones and asked his son to juggle. After a long time, Thomas started getting frustrated and tired. Soon the stones fell frequently, and the juggling ended. "Juggling is weary work," his father said. "It is much easier to just hold on to a stone, or even to pass a stone or two from hand to hand. But to juggle demands attention, care, and even craft. Juggling is more than a science; it is an art. It is both hard work and a source of great joy and wonder."

∽

Thomas sat down for a moment and looked at the steeple below. He felt that there was still a piece missing. He looked at his father and asked, "How does Jesus Christ become the focus of Christian community?"

His father looked down on the church. High on the steeple, the sun reflected off a gold cross. They both knew the meaning of this symbol. The cross announced that the community gathered here was united, bound together by the life, death, and resurrection of Jesus Christ.

"Just how does Jesus fit into God's passion to be in relationship with the world and God's unending presence in and through Word?" the son asked as he followed his father's gaze.

Looking at the cross, Thomas listened to his father.

∽

The people got tired of juggling. Their weariness led to a deafness to Word. The people lost the wonder and joy of living in the dynamic tension. They were consumed with its opposite: despair and hopelessness. God seemed distant and Word silenced.

But God did not grow weary, and God's Word would not be silenced. God's passion to be in a relationship of vulnerable love would not be quieted. So God again spoke, like God spoke at creation, and to Abraham, and at the Exodus, and in the wilderness, and through priests, kings, and prophets. God spoke Word more clearly than ever before. In speaking, God became more vulnerable, and secured a promised presence even death could not end.

God sent God's self in the form of a son, the Word made flesh. His name is Jesus. In Jesus, God's unrelenting fervor to be in relationship with God's creation was made visible, present, and alive.

Jesus embodied the three characteristics that shaped God's vision for God's people.[13] Jesus is the Savior who brings life and hope to all the world. In him, life abundant becomes a reality. In Jesus, it is possible to have freedom, meaning, purpose, and peace beyond understanding. Embraced by the love of Jesus and his vision, one can only respond, as did the Hebrews of old, in bold acts of praise.

Jesus comes and dwells on earth as the One who inaugurates the reign of God. Jesus is ruler and invites people to order their lives as part of this vision of the kingdom. Jesus calls all people to be disciples, followers, who walk the way of his vision. They are invited to live into and out of the story and to practice a life of faithful obedience. Jesus becomes righteousness for God's people. In and through Jesus, all people are made right with their God and with each other. Such a right relationship leads to a life of reconciliation and right ordering (right in relationship to God's vision) of the world.

And Jesus makes God's profound compassion flesh and blood. The Savior of the world and the One who inaugurates the reign of God turns the world upside down. It is not the powerful and the mighty who will one day be victorious; it is the humble, the hungry, the poor, the outcast. Jesus comes not to temples, houses, or thrones of mighty rulers. Jesus comes, born into poverty and living a vulnerable life, dwelling with outsiders, strangers, and the forgotten. His commitment to the children, women, Gentiles, and the sick and disturbed illustrate that he is an incarnate expression of God's radical compassion.

God sent Word into the world as flesh and blood. This Word, comprised of praise, righteousness, and compassion, has a name, a history, a life. Word entered the world as Jesus. And the greatest miracle of all is that though the world tried to silence this Word, tried to resolve the tension, tried to once and for all end God's passionate pursuit of God's creation, they could not. Not even death could end the vision. Jesus, who died on a cross, rose again and lives even today.

Today there are disciples who bear the mark of the cross as a sign of hope. For the cross reminds them that the dynamic tension will not be resolved. The juggling act will continue. Those who are washed into this life of juggling and who bear the mark of the cross will be a people who will always be involved in living the dynamic tension of praise, righteousness, and compassion. And, in order to hold it all together, they seek to keep their focus on Jesus, the Word made flesh.

❧

Thomas picked up three rocks and put them in his pocket. He mumbled to himself: praise, righteousness, compassion. The afternoon was coming to an end, so they began heading home. Walking quietly, each thought of new ways they were called to be part of a peculiar people.

The next few years the two of them occasionally hiked up the hill. At times, as they looked down upon the church below, they would continue to explore the nature of God's gathered people.

They had conversations about the Trinity and how this picture of God, three-in-one, informed and shaped the views of the people of God. God is a community living a dynamic tension between three characteristics. God the Father is creator and the source of order—righteousness. God the Son is Savior and the source of abundant life and hope—praise. God the Spirit is one whose breath instills new insight and vision, and thus opens the people to the outsider, the stranger, and especially the poor and forgotten—compassion.

They spoke of church history and how the church has struggled to keep juggling these three characteristics in a dynamic tension. They recounted time after time when God's people gave in to the temptation to embrace only one or two characteristics. They reviewed how when this happened God's Word again broke into the world and reminded the people to keep juggling, not to be wearied by the struggle, and to keep their focus on Jesus, the vision incarnate.

Often as they talked, Thomas juggled stones. It was his nature, his character, to be an artist.

༁

A few years later, as a sophomore in college, Thomas was sitting at a planning meeting for a campus ministry group. The question they were discussing was, "What will be the focus of our activity this coming year?" He heard the question as a creation question. He asked himself, "How are we to be?"

One of the group said that they must focus on Bible study, prayer, and worship. Another thought that what was needed was an opportunity to deepen friendships and to learn how to relate to each other in healthy ways. Yet another spoke up and said, "We must do servant projects and get involved with those who are in need."

Thomas sat and listened and began to juggle a pencil, chalk, and an eraser. When there was a lull and everyone had started looking at him, he spoke. "All three. To be a faithful community, we must juggle all three. That is the nature of God's people. That is what makes us who we are."

They looked at him and at the continuous movement of the juggling before them. In a voice that sounded almost hypnotized, one of them said, "Huh?"

Thomas did not let this put him off or distract him from his focus. He kept juggling and started to tell them the story: a story of God's people and how they came to be who they are.

He began, "*Word!* A spoken word moved over the chaos and brought forth a people. *Word!* An alien Word, that is from outside, from beyond, from some other sphere. *Word!* It implied a relationship, a hearing, an other who would respond. *Word!* God spoke and in this Word, which is breath with meaning, God's Spirit settled upon all that was and "called, gathered, and enlightened and makes holy the whole Christian church." It all began and it has all continued with *Word!*"

12

THE ISLAND OF FAITHFULNESS

The Invitation

In the ocean of life, in the sea of experience, exists an island: the Island of Faithfulness. The island has a peculiar climate; an environment unique among other solid landforms thrives amid the fluid water. The island has a character that often leaves its mark upon those who explore the terrain.

The invitation arrives in a simple form: come. Come and traverse this island, the Island of Faithfulness. Come and wander along the Way. Come and pilgrimage among the surroundings. Like most adventures, this journey will change you, will touch you. You will be made new.

Evangelism begins with an invitation: an invitation to journey on the Island of Faithfulness.

The Voyage

Arriving at the Island of Faithfulness requires a voyage through the seas. No one arrives on the shores without first crossing the waters. The tastes and smells of the sea accompany each traveler as if they are essential baggage.

Over the years, the seas have changed. Now the waters reflect a certain condition, a context. For anyone who would venture forth to the Island of Faithfulness, there can be no escaping the context.

The current of shame runs deep. This quiet yet powerful flow draws into its movement all that voyages upon its water. Only a willful directness can intercede against the pressure of shame's pull. Deep waters of shame shape the context: Shame for what has been. Shame for the present. Shame for what the future likely holds. Shame runs deeper than guilt. Guilt has to do with what one does, but shame has to do with who one is. The seas are made dangerous by turbulent currents of shame. All who arrive at the Island of Faithfulness come riding this tide. The contemporary North American (Canada and the United States) context provides no escape from this reality.

Waves of fear beat against all who venture over the seas. Fear, a reaction to the increasing intensity and occurrence of violence, marks all who arrive upon the shores of the Island of Faithfulness. The fear expresses itself in anxiety. Anxiety produces a lack of adaptability. Those who accept the invitation for the adventure often come afraid, anxious, and closed to any experiences of newness. Beaten by the waves, they are weary and exhausted. For many, simply disembarking at the island requires unbelievable courage.

Accompanying the current of shame and the waves of fear are the winds of disappointment. So often on the journey toward the Island of Faithfulness those invited have followed the winds, only to end lost and forsaken. So often, what seemed a gentle breeze of life left them either marooned on a quiet sea or blown off course into chaotic waters. The winds of disappointment have etched the faces of those who long to see a future. Now their skin is rough and dried, their vision cynical. Their trust in destiny is blown free like a kite untethered and is left adrift in the wind.

All who offer the invitation to be pilgrims to the Island of Faithfulness must be aware of the context shaping all who arrive. Shame, fear, and disappointment characterize those who make the voyage. This context cannot be escaped. Evangelists offer the invitation in the midst of this reality.

The Island of Faithfulness

What does this Island of Faithfulness look like? What kind of terrain will pilgrims traverse on this journey? For those who have the courage to make the pilgrimage, what climate will permeate the adventure?

The Island of Faithfulness holds in unity three different topographical and climatic expressions. Those who journey on the Island of Faithfulness will be exposed to three different expressions of life. The full character of the island cannot be experienced without exposure to all three.

The Valley of Righteousness

Upon arrival on the island, most adventurers seek out the place most comfortable and available to them. Those who journey over the seas of shame, fear, and disappointment first usually seek out the Valley of Righteousness. The path traveled to this valley is well worn from the many who have scurried down it in anticipation of what they will receive.

Often those who travel the path to the Valley of Righteousness ask what it means. What is righteousness? Those who guide them on the journey explain that it is a place of right ordering. In the Valley of Righteousness, organization and rules mark the culture. The management of life consumes most of the energy of those who dwell there. The assumption undergirding the Valley of Righteousness asserts a mechanistic view of life. Everything can be fixed if the right knowledge, right understanding, right rules, and right orders can be found and followed. The valley's civilization relies on techniques, programs, and other helpful ways for making life work.

It is no wonder that those who arrive on the Island of Faithfulness quickly proceed to the Valley of Righteousness. For those fragmented by the chaos of fear, disappointment, and shame, a place of order teeming with the promise of fixing what is broken touches their deepest longings. Could such a place truly exist? Could it be true?

Deep in the Valley of Righteousness stands a strong brick building. The structure houses books. Wisdom literature fills its shelves. Worn from careful study, the book of Proverbs and the latter pastoral epistles hold prominent places on the desks of scholars. A picture of Jesus teaching the disciples dominates the front wall. The basement rooms bustle with activity. People gather for classes and small-group experiences dealing with issues about how to live a happier, more holistic, healthy life. The information shared meets the common needs of those who gather.

The Valley of Righteousness relieves people's anxiety, provides structure for their lives, and provides resources to meet their everyday needs.

Often, however, people soon find themselves restless. The Valley of Righteousness, so useful and relevant, becomes confining. They gaze up at the paths leading to other parts of the Island of Faithfulness. Somehow, the focus on fixing one's own life and dealing with one's own problems becomes claustrophobic. The promised meaning implied in the invitation offered by the Valley of Righteousness never fully materializes. As one problem is fixed, another rises up. When one insight is learned, another teaching is offered. Most importantly, after dwelling in the Valley of Righteousness for some time, people often realize that the fears, hurts, and problems that haunt them most cannot be fixed. The problem of death especially continues to plague them. No one has developed a program, technique, or how-to system to escape this crisis. In fact, in the Valley of Righteousness, death rarely becomes the subject of conversation. What can't be fixed often becomes denied. When people find denial no longer tolerable, they begin to look for another way to journey. There must be more to the Island of Faithfulness than just the Valley of Righteousness.

The packing begins. Those who sojourn on the Island of Faithfulness keep their packs light, putting just a few items in a backpack. As people pack, they carry some remembrances from the Valley of Righteousness. They pack a book, the Bible. The teachings and insights provide a structure and assist in quieting their anxieties when things become frightening. The Bible, used so regularly in the Valley of Righteousness, falls open to the well-read passages of the teachings of Jesus and the prophets of old. In addition to the Bible, proverbial sayings and insights are written in cryptic form and packed away. Lists for managing life and finding fulfillment are collected. Pictures and notes from significant teachers, mentors, and fellow inhabitants in the Valley of Righteousness nest in an envelope. Much has been learned in the Valley of Righteousness, and it will be remembered. Many close relationships have been made, and they will continue to shape those who travel on. Now, with backpack secured, the pilgrimage to other parts of the Island of Faithfulness continues.

The Meadow of Praise

Many paths lead from the Valley of Righteousness, yet those who journey will find themselves in one of two new locations. Either they will discover the Meadow of Praise or the Canyon of Compassion.

The trails toward the Meadow of Praise cover a variety of terrain. Those who make this journey often wonder what lies ahead. Portions of the pilgrimage lead through patches of thick fog. Sounds echo loudly in the heavy clouds that close around the pilgrims. The way ahead demands trust and faith. The route into the Meadow of Praise explores mystery. Often travelers can be seen clutching their backpacks, searching for a how-to book or a manual about organizing mystery. Finally, however, no such resource is available. To enter the Meadow of Praise, people must surrender control and venture into the unknown. Sometimes the cadre of travelers can be seen holding hands, leading each other, coaching one another as they move, step by step, ever deeper into mysterious landscapes.

For many, this portion of the journey on the Island of Faithfulness provides the greatest challenge. Mystery, loss of control, and trust are not characteristics often nurtured. Those who lead this portion of the exploration of the Island of Faithfulness must do so carefully. A gracious balance between appropriate challenge and support is needed. Ultimately, however, the voyagers must step into the meadow, accepting the beauty and grace of the meadow as true gifts.

Those who make this sojourn finally walk through a thick stand of tall pines and enter a large meadow full of plush grass and patches of brilliant wild flowers. The Meadow of Praise commands a sense of awe. Those who enter know this place to be a gift. Wonder, beauty, and glory mark this place. Immediately, vision, spirits, and voices are drawn up to new heights. The radiant sun shines down, and those who gather in the Meadow of Praise bask in its warmth and brilliance. The splendor of the Meadow of Praise has a name. All who wander in this meadow know that God, the God of Jesus Christ, is proclaimed in this beauty. The light shining amid the fog and shadows of the world bears the name of the crucified and risen Lord and Savior, Jesus.

Dwelling in the Meadow of Praise involves living exposed to the sun. At first, after coming through the fog and mystery, the sun seems a welcome friend. Initial life in the meadow involves great joy. People gather to sing songs of praise and thanksgiving to the God who gives life and hope. They clap, dance, and rejoice for the gift given them in this wondrous meadow. There is an order to their celebrations, yet surprises are common. Who knows what new gift will be given? Who knows what novel splendor will break forth? Anticipation and expectation mark the Meadow of Praise. God continually does new things. The response to God's new endeavors is one of praise and thanksgiving.

Over time, inhabitants of the Meadow of Praise find themselves exposed to the radiant glory that comes from above in another way. The light not only comforts and brings warmth; it also reveals truth. In the light, no one can hide. The gift of Jesus not only offers new life, but it calls for transformation and change.

Those who come to the Meadow of Praise find themselves not only looking up to heaven, but also drawn inward. Introspection, confession, contrition, and repentance are common activities for those in the meadow. Living in the light, no denial is possible.

Laments, cries of anguish, prayers of intercession, and other appeals of the soul resound in the meadow. Praise, which most often begins looking up, often turns inward and outward. The Meadow of Praise invites connections with feelings and failings as well as with other brothers and sisters. Praise, which at first seems to draw people away from the present world, compels a return to the world as we know it.

Two areas of the Meadow of Praise are well visited. Upon arriving in the meadow, people usually visit the pool of running water. Cool and refreshing, the water reflects the light of Jesus. Bathing in the pool of water initiates people into the Meadow of Praise. Cleansed and made new, those baptized claim a new name and a new sense of belonging. This new identity stems from the name above all names, Jesus Christ.

Throughout life in the meadow, not just upon arrival, people return repeatedly to the water of life. Sometimes the return derives from a need to remember their name, their identity, so easily forgotten. Other times, people gather at the water to hold each other in a common bond of unity, especially when other forces seem to drive them apart. At still other times, the exposure to the light of Christ reveals deep hurts, failures, and sin. A return to the waters of baptism offers the gift of forgiveness and regeneration.

The Meadow of Praise also hosts great and wonderful feasts. Meals call the people together for nourishment and fellowship. The meals occasion storytelling, caregiving, and profound community-building. All feasts in the Meadow of Praise are fashioned on the meal of the Eucharist—thanksgiving. The Eucharist consists of bread and wine digested with the words and promise: this is the body and blood of Jesus. Praise and thanksgiving involve eating just as living involves breathing. The people who journey to the Meadow of Praise know the axiom to be true: You are what you eat.

A pilgrimage around the Island of Faithfulness must include the Meadow of Praise. Despite its beauty, comfort, and joy, one cannot remain in the meadow. The journey must continue. There is more to the sojourn of the faithful than basking in the light, being washed in the waters, and being fed on the meal of life.

So the pilgrims again pack their backpacks. From the Meadow of Praise, they bring a candle, water, and a cup and plate. In order to venture forth, these items must be present. Although they will leave the Meadow of Praise, its memory must be held tight for nourishment on the journey ahead.

The Canyon of Compassion

At first, the trail out of the Meadow of Praise rises gently. The smell of the flowers, the warmth of the light, and the soft carpet of grass often make those who spend time in the meadow unwary. Soon, however, the trail becomes steep, rocky, and treacherous. The next stop on the Island of Faithfulness is at the end of a diffi-cult and bruising trail. The Canyon of Compassion stands in the way of the pilgrims. In order to experience the whole Island of Faithfulness, people must climb down into the Canyon of Compassion. The descent is risky and challenging. Often the trails are not walked. Rock slides must be traversed. Ankles are easily turned. Legs and arms may be bruised. Those who make this journey experience vulnerability and pain.

The trail leads deeper and deeper into the canyon. The farther down the trail, the more the heat of the day collects and the less the breeze blows. Plunging into the Canyon of Compassion is hard, risky, and challenging work.

Once in the canyon, sounds echo off the stark and steep rock walls. Cries of the hurt, hopeless, forsaken, and forgotten resound. The hungry, imprisoned, abused, neglected, and oppressed shout into the caverns. There is no escape. The sounds are deafening.

Pilgrims, driven to their knees by the cries of anguish, cup their hands over their ears. But the sounds cannot, will not be quieted. Finally, the hands of those who accept the challenge to enter the Canyon of Compassion come together and fold themselves in postures of prayer. And pray they do. Prayer is the beginning of compassion—prayer for those who hurt and know the harsh cruelty of life, prayer for those who experience the absence of God, and prayer for those who wonder if life, abundant life, is possible at all.

In the posture of prayer, the wailing of the whole creation takes on a new tone. For a new voice is added to the chorus of anguish: God's voice. Intoned in the life and death of Jesus, it does not resolve the dissonance. Rather, the wailing of God somehow, mysteriously, holds these cries together and composes them into a wholeness that speaks of hope. In a strange and profound way, listening to the torment of the world opens the ears of the pilgrims to the passion of God.

Those who hazard the journey into the Canyon of Compassion leave changed. Every cry, every hurt, every tear, every longing unfulfilled, resonates in their minds and souls as did the echoes in the canyon. No longer can they deny the hurts around them. No longer can they forget the forgotten. No longer can they live while forsaking the opportunity to reach out to those in need. Also, no longer can they forget the amazing yet dissonant sound of hope they heard. In the Canyon of Compassion, Jesus touched them and opened their hearts to a new way of listening and being.

Weary from the changes they have experienced and the bombardment of hurt they have heard, the pilgrims pack to leave the Canyon of Compassion. In their backpacks, they place stones from the trail. The stones remind them of the hardness of life and the burdens many bear. The stones, unpacked, form an altar upon which the pilgrims can focus their prayers. Stacked carefully, the stones from the Canyon of Compassion cry out in the pains of a creation in travail. These cries call the pilgrims to prayer and acts of compassion.

Pilgrimage on the Island of Faithfulness

The invitation is intended for all people, both congregational members and those yet to be members, to enter more deeply into Jesus and the community that bears his name. Or to continue our metaphor, all people are invited to wander around the Island of Faithfulness. Discipleship, following Jesus, summons people to be pilgrims. The call to follow Jesus means sojourning and being part of a movement. The early Christians were called "people of the way." Today, being the church means venturing forth in new directions.

This call to wander on the Island of Faithfulness is not a call to an aimless jaunt. The island has places that must be visited. Praise, righteousness, and compassion are the characteristics that must not be forgotten. All three must be present in a voyage of discipleship. None can be denied.

Those who journey on the Island of Faithfulness continually experience the temptation to settle down and make a home in one place or another. For some, the Valley of Righteousness will be the homestead, a place of order, security, and careful living. Others might seek out a home in the Meadow of Praise, a beautiful place where eyes are turned to heaven and the struggles and pains of the world are forgotten. Still others, activists who insist that all real faith must be active in love, might be energized and seek to make an encampment in the Canyon of Compassion. Whenever God's people forsake the call to be pilgrims, they lose their faithful perspective. God's people are on the move. Evangelism invites people to go on the road, to traverse the island, to continually explore one part of it after another.

Offering such an invitation in the present context provides a tremendous challenge. People who are shamed, afraid, and disappointed tend not to be adventuresome. We long for a place to be coddled, entertained, and held. We often look for a place with secure walls, locked doors, and easily accessible happiness. Shame encourages us to feel inadequate. Fear makes us turn from all but the familiar and safe. Disappointment turns us inward, for we cannot trust anyone but ourselves.

The community of faith must not let this context set the agenda. The church must withstand the temptation to focus on these needs to the exclusion of the invitation to be part of the whole pilgrimage. To subvert the gospel and call people to discipleship in this way will finally not serve either the people or the faithful witness to Jesus. We must, with all our imagination and compassion, invite people to journey around the whole Island of Faithfulness. Only such a pilgrimage will lead to real joy, hope, and life. Anything less will leave us ashamed, afraid, and disappointed yet again.

The Church's Invitation to the World

All are welcome. Come on the adventure to the Island of Faithfulness. The voyage over the seas of the present context may be difficult, but the journey is worth it. Once on the island, you are likely to find some places you enjoy more than others. But you must pilgrimage to praise, righteousness, and compassion. You will at times get weary and seek to settle down and make a home, but the adventure of faith demands being on the way.

This is the promise. You will know great joy and abundant life. The journey you will take is the good news of hope in Jesus Christ. God will provide what you need. You will not be disappointed.

All are welcome! Come on the adventure to the Island of Faithfulness. Come.

AFTERWORD

What I have offered in these pages is not a strategy, certainly not a road map, and all who look for a plan with goals and objectives are likely disappointed. In fact, I propose that all such means of dealing with the reality of contemporary congregational life are ineffective, and more importantly, lack the depth of faith needed to sustain the church in its witness.

Instead, I have been inviting congregations to move beyond the church-growth principles that so dominate congregational life in North America. The time has come to set aside the many modern trappings that I believe significantly inhibit the gospel witness. Congregations and their leaders must risk venturing forward, trusting God to lead them, and daring to surrender, not to a plan or a strategy, but to a relationship and the vision that relationship sustains. A congregation that moves beyond church growth will find itself envisioning a life radically centered on God and graciously called to serve the world.

Where this relationship will lead cannot be known. What will be the specific practice of congregations in this newly emerging world? No one is certain. How can congregations and their leaders prepare for the adventure to which they are called? One way, among others, must be proposed. The church must prepare through prayer.

Most mornings I begin my day by praying "A Prayer for the Beginning of the Day." As the church moves beyond church growth into a new day, this prayer might be a source of comfort, courage, and support. It has been claimed that the prayer originates from a

Russian Orthodox metropolitan in Moscow around 1000 C.E.
Notice that this prayer is not a plan or a strategy. The prayer calls
us to relinquish ourselves to God and allow God to direct, teach,
and guide us as we move into the new day.

I am convinced praying and living into this prayer will move
us beyond church growth.

> O Lord, grant me to meet the coming days in peace.
>
> Help me in all things to rely upon thy holy will.
>
> In every hour of the day reveal thy will to me.
>
> Bless my dealings with all who surround me.
>
> Teach me to treat all that comes to me throughout the day with
>> peace of soul,
>>
>> and the firm conviction thy will governs all.
>
> In all my deeds and words guide my thoughts and feelings.
>
> In unforeseen events let me not forget that all are sent by thee.
>
> Teach me to act firmly and wisely, without embittering or
>> embarrassing others.
>
> Give me the strength to bear the fatigue of the coming day and
>> all it shall bring.
>
> Direct my will, teach me to pray, pray thou thyself in me.
>
> Amen.

Notes

Introduction

1. Gerhard O. Forde, *Where God Meets Man: Luther's Down-to-Earth Approach to the Gospel* (Minneapolis: Augsburg, 1972), 43.

2. Douglas John Hall, *The Future of the Church: Where Are We Headed?* (Toronto: United Church Publishing House, 1989). Written for the Canadian Church, the book provides an accessible and personal account of the demise of Christendom. A more thorough and academic appraisal can be found in Douglas John Hall's three-volume systematics: *Thinking the Faith: Christian Theology in a North American Context* (Minneapolis: Fortress Press, 1991); *Professing the Faith: Christian Theology in a North American Context* (Minneapolis: Fortress Press, 1993); *Confessing the Faith: Christian Theology in a North American Context* (Minneapolis: Fortress Press, 1996).

3. Among the many authors who discuss this reality, the following have been most helpful in the formation of my understanding: Susan Bordo, *The Flight of Objectivity: Essays on Cartesianism and Culture* (Albany, N.Y.: State Univ. of New York Press, 1987); Albert Borgmann, *Crossing the Postmodern Divide* (Chicago: Univ. of Chicago Press, 1992); Stanley J. Grentz, *A Primer on Postmodernism* (Grand Rapids: Eerdmans, 1996); Stephen Toulmin, *Cosmopolis: The Hidden Agenda of Modernity* (Chicago: Univ. of Chicago Press, 1990).

4. William Strauss and Neil Howe, *The Fourth Turning: An American Prophecy* (New York: Broadway, 1997).

5. The following provide a few of the voices calling for new imagination beyond the modern agenda: Walter Brueggemann, *Cadences of Home: Preaching among Exiles* (Louisville, Ky.: Westminster John Knox, 1997); and *Texts under Negotiation: The Bible and Postmodern Imagination* (Minneapolis: Fortress Press, 1993); Douglas John Hall, *Thinking the Faith; idem, Professing the Faith; idem, Confessing the Faith*; the work of the Gospel and Our Culture Network, George R. Hunsberger and Craig Van Gelder, eds., *The Church between Gospel and Culture: The Emerging Mission in North America* (Grand Rapids:

Eerdmans, 1996); and Craig Van Gelder, ed., *Confident Witness—Changing World: Rediscovering the Gospel in North America*, Gospel and Our Culture Network (Grand Rapids: Eerdmans, 1999).

6. Albert Borgmann, *Crossing the Postmodern Divide* (Chicago: Univ. of Chicago Press, 1992), 27–33.

7. *Lutheran Book of Worship* (Minneapolis: Augsburg Fortress, 1978), 153.

Chapter 1

1. The delineation of these ten pieces has as its source the work of Stanley J. Grenz, *A Primer on Postmodernism* (Grand Rapids: Eerdmans, 1996), 2–4.

2. The story of Réne Descartes and its implications for modernity is wonderfully told by Stephen Toulmin, *Cosmopolis: The Hidden Agenda of Modernity* (Chicago: Univ. of Chicago Press, 1990).

3. The German theologian Eberhard Jungel describes this well in *God as the Mystery of the World: On the Foundation of the Theology of the Crucified One in the Dispute between Theism and Atheism* (Grand Rapids: Eerdmans, 1983). "The world forces itself into God's place, as the world of man. That means, then, that modern man can no longer distance himself from the contradictions and nihilisms around him. . . . Rather, modern man is responsible for 'his' world. That is how he experiences himself. He experiences thus his failure, his guilt, and even his misfortune as the worldly consequences of his own actions. . . . Man burdens the world with himself, and thus the world becomes too weighty" (52).

4. See Edwin H. Friedman, *A Failure of Nerve: Leadership in the Age of the Quick Fix* (Bethesda, Md.: Edwin Friedman Estate, 1999), chap. 3, "Data Junkyards and Data Junkies: The Fallacy of Expertise," 127–73.

5. A phrase and concept used often by Kennon L Callahan, *Twelve Keys to an Effective Church: Strategic Planning for Mission* (San Francisco, Harper and Row, 1983).

6. See Edward Farley, *Theologia: The Fragmentation and Unity of Theological Education* (Philadelphia: Fortress Press, 1983).

7. See Douglas John Hall, *Thinking the Faith: Christian Theology in a North American Context* (Minneapolis: Augsburg, 1989), 158–68.

8. See Walter Wink, *The Bible and Human Transformation: Toward a New Paradigm for Biblical Study* (Philadelphia: Fortress Press, 1973).

Chapter 2

1. Paul D. Hanson, *The People Called: The Growth of Community in the Bible* (San Francisco: Harper and Row, 1986), 253.

2. This is the theme of the book by Douglas John Hall, *The Future of the Church: Where Are We Headed?* (Toronto: United Church, 1989).

Chapter 3

1. *With One Voice: A Lutheran Resource for Worship* (Minneapolis: Augsburg Fortress, 1995).

Chapter 5

1. A good resource is Gail Ramshaw, *Between Sundays: Daily Bible Readings Based on the Revised Common Lectionary* (Minneapolis: Augsburg Fortress, 1997).

Chapter 8

1. Robert G. Hamerton-Kelly, *Sacred Violence: Paul's Hermeneutic of the Cross* (Minneapolis: Fortress Press, 1992).

2. Ibid., 20.

3. Ibid., 20–21.

4. Ibid., 21.

Chapter 9

1. See Walter Brueggemann, *The Prophetic Imagination* (Philadelphia: Fortress Press, 1978).

2. James McGregor Burns, *Leadership* (New York: Harper, 1978). Burns writes: "Leaders, whatever their professions of harmony, do not shun conflict; they confront it, exploit it, and ultimately embody it" (39).

3. Robert Fritz, *The Path of Least Resistance: Learning to Become the Creative Force in Your Own Life* (New York: Fawcett Columbine, 1984).

4. Mark A. Olson, *The Evangelical Pastor: Pastoral Leadership for a Witnessing People* (Minneapolis: Augsburg, 1989), 9.

5. See Gerhard Lohfink, *Jesus and Community* (Philadelphia: Fortress Press, 1984).

6. William H. Willimon, *Calling and Character: Virtues of the Ordained Life* (Nashville: Abingdon, 2000), 107.

Chapter 11

1. When one enters deeply into questions of being, one moves toward myth. Myth has to do with questions of meaning and purpose,

and thus deals not primarily with practical concerns, but with the context in which practice takes place. "Myth was regarded as primary; it was concerned with what was thought to be timeless and constant in our existence. . . . Myth was not concerned with practical matters, but with meaning. . . . The various mythological stories, which were not intended to be taken literally, were an ancient form of psychology. When people told stories about heroes who descended to the underworld, struggled through labyrinths, or fought with monsters, they were bringing to light the obscure regions of the subconscious realm, which is not accessible to purely rationalistic investigation, but which has a profound effect upon our experience and behavior." Karen Armstrong, *The Battle for God* (New York: Knopf, 2000), xiii.

2. Story provides a way for God's people to participate in God's act of creation and redemption. "In the resurrection community in which Christians live in the presence of the risen Lord and by the guidance of the Holy Spirit, there is no fixed code of moral absolutes. . . . We live and walk by the Spirit, and therefore we must strive to find a meaningful place for all persons in this new community. Each is given his role, but the precise lines that he speaks are not given—he must contribute freely and creatively to the story." Robert Roth, *Story and Reality: An Essay on Truth* (Grand Rapids: Eerdmans, 1973), 196.

3. "Thus one main reason why we read Scripture is so that we may not settle easily for any other notion of life, forgetting who we are and the understanding of life that we have confessed and embraced. Informed by the Bible, we are invited to live in faithful response to this faithful covenant partner. . . . In other words, one of the most important gifts the Bible can give us is a frame of reference for our lives." Walter Brueggemann, *The Bible Makes Sense* (Atlanta: John Knox, 1977), 17.

4. Leonardo Boff, *Holy Trinity, Perfect Community*, trans. Philip Berryman (Maryknoll, N.Y.: Orbis, 2000).

5. Robert Kolb and Timothy J. Wengert, eds., *The Book of Concord: The Confessions of the Evangelical Lutheran Church* (Minneapolis: Fortress Press, 2000), 355.

6. See Gustaf Wingren, *The Living Word: A Theological Study of Preaching and the Church* (Philadelphia: Fortress Press, 1960).

7. See Dietrich Bonhoeffer, *Creation and Fall: A Theological Interpretation of Genesis 1–3* (New York: Macmillan, 1959).

8. Jack Miles, *God: A Biography* (New York: Knopf, 1995), 58–61.

9. See Paul D. Hanson, *The People Called: The Growth of Community in the Bible* (San Francisco: Harper and Row, 1986), 5. "We shall see especially that a unique triadic notion of community persists from earliest

Yahwistic times down through the early rabbinical and Christian period. The understanding of the righteousness, compassion, and worship that characterizes this triad and defines the realm of *shalom* to which God invites the faithful to live undergoes constant change. Yet, its persistence over the centuries can be taken as testimony to the trustworthiness of the Bible as a guide for those communities of faith that today seek to bring all humans to the fullness of life that seems to be in harmony with our deepest spiritual insights."

10. Daniel W. Erlander, *Manna and Mercy: A Brief History of God's Unfolding Promise to Mend the Entire Universe* (Mercer Island, Wash.: The Order of Saints Martin and Teresa, 1992), 7–9.

11. Folk song based on the Song of Miriam, Exodus 15.

12. Walter Brueggemann, *The Creative Word: Canon as a Model for Biblical Education* (Philadelphia: Fortress Press, 1982).

13. In addition to the classic description of Jesus as priest, king, and prophet, Marcus Borg speaks of him as Revitalization Movement Founder, Sage, and Prophet. Marcus Borg, *Jesus, a New Vision: Spirit, Culture, and the Life of Discipleship* (San Francisco: Harper and Row, 1987).